Saturn and Oth

Edwin Moi

Text of the opening lecture from Writing Together, *Glasgow, April 1990*

When I was asked to provide a title for my talk, as the programme was being printed, long before I knew what I was going to say, I was thinking of my book *From Glasgow to Saturn,* which was being used as an overall title for the conference; that book contains poems about Glasgow, but also about Saturn and other worlds real and imaginary. The poem which mentions Saturn is about an abortive mission to 'the rings of Saturn'. But now, of course, we have had a *real* mission, by the American Voyager spacecraft, to the rings of Saturn and beyond, and we have had sent back an amazing series of photographs of the outer planets of the solar system. Well, that set my mind going, in a much less controlled way than that of the Voyager probe, and I thought about all those newly-discovered rings and satellites - three new moons for Jupiter, six new moons for Neptune, seven new moons for Saturn, ten new moons for Uranus - *and* Neptune has three rings, Uranus has ten rings, while Saturn has five hundred rings! The Earth, with one satellite and no rings at all, seems very poorly furnished, a sort of peahen among all the peacocks. But then I thought how the Earth has made up for it by having so many rings and satellites within its own boundaries, in its countries and organisations and laws and languages, and I begin to feel the stirrings of a theme which might link me to this week's activities.

But how far can we speak of 'the Earth' as a unit, as an entity? It is noticeable that there have been no *Earth* expeditions to the moon (whether by man or by machines), only American or Russian; there are already items in Roman and Cyrillic script lying on the surface of the moon, and if the Japanese, who are likely to be next, drop or leave something in Japanese script, any galactic observers might be puzzled: how come Earth persons have no world government, if their technology is good enough to send rockets to the moon? Indeed they may not think very much of us at all, if we believe the Italian poet Montale, who has a short poem called 'Joviana':

> Billions of poems are written
> on Earth but it is very different on Jupiter.
> Not a single line is created. Of course
> Jovian scholarship is something else.
> What it is no one knows. All we do know
> is that on that world the human tongue is
> hilarious.

Perhaps the inhabitants of Jupiter are so jovial that they cannot help laughing at our backward Earth with its primitive speech and fumbling poetry. But if we are backward, backward in our social and political organisation, so that it was impossible for us to send a United Nations rocket for the first moon landing, instead of (as happened) having the Stars & Stripes planted in the lunar dust, like an atavistic sign of conquest (and that remains true, despite the astronaut's remark about 'a giant leap for mankind'), if we are still so bound by feelings of territory and domination that we take a national flag to the moon, or like the Russians drop a Soviet plaque from an orbiting probe to show that they too were there, is this a good thing or a bad thing? Are we really all that backward, or on the contrary is this how evolution proceeds, through diversity, endless diversity with all its attendant dangers and difficulties? These are basic questions.

The world is a sphere (well, nearly). A sphere is a very satisfying shape; it seems to enclose, to make things manageable and hold them together. Both the sphere and the circle also suggest power. There are spheres of influence, ruling circles, satellite countries. An alchemist would draw a magic circle round himself to call up supernatural forces. Prehistoric stone circles, often concentric like the rings of the outer planets, were also places of power, whether for religious ritual or as early astronomical observatories. Dancing in a ring was an expression of group solidarity. The hundred and fifty knights of the Arthurian Round Table, when they sat in solemn conclave round their enormous circular table, were a force to be reckoned with, and when the Round Table was dissolved, and the knights with their chivalric ideals were all killed or scattered, it seemed like the end of the world. But it wasn't. As the dying King Arthur reminds us in Tennysons's *Idylls of the King*: "The old order changeth, yielding place to new . . . Lest one good custom should corrupt the world." So the Round Table had to go, just as the beautiful concentric spheres of the old Ptolemaic astronomy had to go. The world not only revolves physically but is in a constant state of change and upheaval, and Tennyson seems to be saying that only through such revolution can a forward or upward movement or momentum be maintained.

So perhaps spheres and circles, despite their attraction, are always ambiguous figures? Louis XIV of France (1638-1715) was called *Le Roi Soleil*, the Sun King. He was at the centre of a solar system of wealth, power, privilege and culture. His rays went out to a cluster of great writers: Corneille, Racine, Moliere. A glittering court revolved round the king, Paris revolved round the court, France revolved round Paris, and (as the king would like to think) the world revolved round France, it made such an impression on other nations. But the Sun King was also a despot who sat like a spider at the centre of a web of corruption; he interfered at will with the courts of justice; and he sent out ring after ring of war and anxiety and disruption among his neighbours in Germany and the Netherlands and Italy and Spain. Some were sorry, but many were glad, when that sun went out.

Is history, therefore, simply telling us to beware of suns and systems, centres and satellites, spheres and circles? The Italian philosopher Vico (1668-1744) looked back at history and saw it as a spiral of recurring but not identical cycles or phases, *corsi e ricorsi*, over huge stretches of time; if we took the long view, a developing pattern would emerge, but it wouldn't be smooth or symmetrical. The reason for this comes from his belief - well ahead of his time - that civilisation had many initial centres, and didn't proceed in a wave of diffusion from one core or source. He saw a succession of three phases, which he called the age of gods, the age of heroes, and the age of men. Ancient Egypt was an age of gods, Ancient Greece an age of

Collected Poems

Edwin Morgan

'Morgan's poetry has always been large, vigorous and imaginative. It has been energetic and various. It has, as critics have wearied themselves telling us, been composed of straight narrative, concrete poetry, sci-fi, satire . . . More than the work of most poets, it welcomes the twentieth century.' Iain Crichton Smith

Edwin Morgan

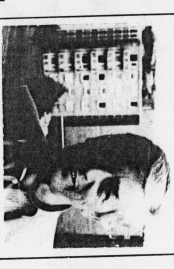

from Carcanet

'The qualities that most appeal are a capacity for celebration . . . and an unsentimental humaneness, a considering sympathy.'
TIMES LITERARY SUPPLEMENT

'Whether he is writing about the relationship of language to nationalism or the theme of metamorphosis in the verse of Andrei Voznesensky, Mr Morgan writes in a way which I would characterise as generous and forceful as well as immediately sensible.'
Robert Nye, *Scotsman*

Crossing the Border

Return to: Carcanet Press, 208 Corn Exchange, Manchester M4 3BQ

Please send me

| | Edwin Morgan - Collected Poems | £25.00 |
| | Edwin Morgan - Crossing the Border | £25.00 |

Also available

	Edwin Morgan - Selected Poems	£4.95
	Sorley MacLean - From Wood to Ridge	£18.95
	Iain Crichton Smith - Selected Stories	£12.95

(Please add £2.00 postage)

I enclose a cheque for £_____, OR charge my Access/Visa account

with £_____.   Card No _____ Expiry ____/____/199__

Signature _____ Name _____

Address _____

Post code _____ Telephone _____

heroes, Ancient Rome an age of men. But there were similar developments before Egypt and after Rome. We hear a lot these days about core and periphery. We see various attacks from the peripheries - Georgia, Azerbaijan, Lithuania - on the hard cores of the world. Vico would argue that every periphery is a potential core - and he should know, a brilliant man living in Naples, a city which was then ruled by non-Italians.

Today, we know that some prehistoric tombs, stone circles and megaliths in Scotland are older, not younger, than similar monuments from the Mediterranean area which were once believed to have inspired them. The western and northern islands of Scotland are about as peripheral to the body of Europe as you can get, but they were also, in their time, a core, a core of great builders who must have had the social organisation (and the language) required to put up these monuments, at dates before the Egyptian pyramids. If Vico had known about carbon dating, he would have loved it. Would he have called the Scottish builders gods, or heroes, or just men?

Scotland, then, takes part in some large circles. There was a human settlement on the island of Rum about 6600 BC, which means that it is older than Rome. Hugh MacDiarmid had a vision of Scotland caught up in a still bigger circle, a sort of Viconian supercircle, in his long poem *A Drunk Man Looks at the Thistle*, when he finds himself, and Scotland, on the rim of the Great Wheel of the cosmos which makes a turn every 26,000 years with the precession of the equinoxes. He doesn't much enjoy the experience:

> Then suddenly I see as weel
> As me spun roon within the wheel,
> The helpless forms o God and Deil.

> And on a birlin edge I see
> Wee Scotland squattin like a flea,
> And dizzy wi the speed, and me! . . .

> But wae's me on the weary wheel!
> Higgledy-piggledy in't we reel,
> And little it cares hoo we may feel.

> Twenty-six thoosan years 't'll tak
> for it to threid the Zodiac
> - A single roon o the wheel to mak!

> Lately it turned - I saw mysel
> In sic a company doomed to mell,
> I micht hae been in Dante's Hell. . .

> I felt it turn, and syne I saw
> John Knox and Clavers in my raw,
> And Mary Queen o Scots anaw,

> And Rabbie Burns and Weelum Wallace,
> And Carlyle lookin unco gallus,
> And Harry Lauder (to enthrall us).

> And as I looked I saw them aw,
> Aw the Scots baith big and smaw,
> That eer the braith o life did draw.

'Mercy o Gode, I canna thole
Wi sic an orra mob to roll.'
- 'Wheesht! It's for the gude o your soul . . .'

MacDiarmid sees history as a vast, slowly turning circle from which he would like to, but cannot, escape; a wheel he likens to one of the circles or *giri* of Dante's *Inferno*. The circle, the wheel, is grand and impressive, but it also suggests something predetermined he wants to break away from by asserting his own irregular spontaneous will. It reminds you of Joyce's *Finnegans Wake*, which may be a circular book, but no circle ever took longer to get closed. And *Finnegans Wake* reminds us, since it is a labyrinthine book, that if circles are ancient symbols of desirability and power, so too are mazes and labyrinths, which in a sense are the opposite of circles. Stephen Dedalus was the hero of Joyce's *A Portrait of the Artist as a Young Man*, and the original Daedalus of legend was the great artist-engineer who designed and built the famous labyrinth on Crete. A maze may have a beginning and end, but you may never reach the end, or may reach it but never find your way back, and its mysteriousness can induce panic as well as pleasure.

I mentioned earlier the importance of dancing in a circle, but in mediaeval times people used also to dance through a maze, which is a less obvious but more interesting thing to do. Both the circle dance and the maze dance were thought to be symbolic of something universal in their different ways. And in the most symbolic dance of all, the profound and wonderful dance of the Dervishes in Turkey, each dancer spins in a circle, with arms outstretched, the left palm facing downwards to embrace the earth and the right palm facing upwards to embrace the heavens, and each dancer spins in his own time, not in unison with the other dancers (though obviously it is a group activity), like the planets of our solar system which we now know are extraordinarily varied, in ways that so far defy logical development or evolution. If you can imagine someone looking down from above on a dance of Dervishes, it would be like the movement of fundamental particles, in the sense that you could never predict exactly where any one dancer would be in relation to the others. And yet some force does hold them together. A nice image of what physicists now call chaos.

So is the world a circle or a labyrinth? Geometry or chaos? We are here this week to speak together, to write together. Our world is, among other things, a world of language. Is language, since the Tower of Babel, more like a labyrinth than anything as ideal as a ring or a sphere? In the 17th century, when European nation-states were establishing themselves, and when Latin was in its death-throes as a means of international communication, many minds were turned to the idea of a new universal language to replace Latin. This was taken up especially in France, England and Scotland. George Dalgarno from Aberdeen (*Ars Signorum*, 1661) and Sir Thomas Urquhart of Cromarty (*Logopandecteision*, 1653) were among the leading lights.

Urquhart, unlike the inventor of Esperanto in more recent times, believed you must start from scratch, it was wrong to be Eurocentric, to have your new language branded as one more attempt by Europe to impose its ideas on the rest of the world. He wanted to have sounds, syllables and words built up according to rational principles, so that once you had learned the basic building-blocks of the language you could tell at a glance what any word meant. Anyone, from any part of the world, could do this. Grammatically, it had twelve parts of speech, eleven cases, and eleven genders (which should cover most eventualities!). In some ways, what he was looking for, before his time, was a computer language, and in our period the interest in interlinguas and universal grammar has been revived, so the seventeenth-century linguists were forerunners of something, though we still don't have our universal language. Urquhart unfortunately never gave any examples of his new language, so we don't know if it was all in his head or whether he had really worked it out on paper in one of his many lost documents. Certainly a universal language wouldn't come amiss. If you saw someone coming towards you and speaking as follows, would you know what to do?

> Agonou dont oussys vou denaguez algarou, nou den farou zamist vous mariston ulbrou, fousquez vou brol, tam bredaguez moupreton den goul houst, daguez daguez nou croupys fost bardounnoflist nou grou. Agou paston tol nalprissys hourton los ecbatonous prou dhouquys brol panygou den bascrou noudous caguous goulfren goul oust troppassou.

That was from Rabelais' *Gargantua and Pantagruel* (Book 2), from the incident where Pantagruel, out walking with his friends, is confronted by a starving man pleading for help, a man who eventually becomes his great friend Panurge. Panurge asks for help in thirteen languages, including Basque and Scots, but also including three different languages invented by Rabelais, of which the passage I quote is one. Panurge does in the end use French and make his wants known. The whole thing is a little fable, which says both 'Oh, if only we had an international language!', and yet at the same time 'Oh, isn't the variety of human speech fascinating and admirable!'

In Britain we tend to think, with some complacency, that English is on its way to becoming *the* world language, not in the sense of displacing existing languages (though it may well happen) but as an auxiliary, second language to be used for international purposes, much as Latin was in the Middle Ages throughout Europe. But we have been reminded recently by the linguist Randolph Quirk that 'in the world as a whole, English remains an exotic tongue to perhaps 90 percent of the population - and the percentage is growing . . . as a matter of demography.' That's a startling thought, but it shows just how open and unpredictable the global language situation is. Languages rise and fall. Nothing is sacrosanct. Some do die out, in the same way as entire nations and civilisations have disappeared. Stateless nations often make their languages a rallying-point, as in the Baltic countries today; yet the unique tongue of the Basques has not helped them to attain statehood. Some languages seem to thrive through periods of suppression, like Hungarian; others, such as Scottish and Irish Gaelic, are less resilient. A language may suddenly start to revive and grow, for reasons that are not clear, like Quechua, spoken by millions of Indians in South America - but could it ever replace Spanish and Portuguese - who knows? The boundaries and strengths of the world's languages are continually shifting and changing, rather like those tectonic plates the continents ride on. Any dreams of unity, any shimmering ideal of a golden sphere of global language which we could take with us when we explore Jupiter and Saturn, seems far away, and might materialise only if a universal mathematical or computer language could first be agreed and then verbalised.

The ideal itself has always been open to scepticism, and some mockery. It's interesting that in the 'rational' eighteenth century, when human reason was being applied to many areas of learning, the great satirist Swift thought it was time to attack the concept of a universal means of communication which had been mooted in the previous century. In *Gulliver's Travels*, in Part 3, his wide-eyed hero visits the Academy of Lagado, a metropolis on the continent of Balnibarbi, and is shown round the school of languages there. Among the projects he is told about, there is one for a universal language:

> The other project was a scheme for entirely abolishing all words whatsoever; and this was urged as a great advantage in point of health as well as brevity. For it is plain that every word we speak is in some degree a diminution of our lungs by corrosion, and consequently contributes to the shortening of our lives. An expedient was therefore offered, that since words are only names for *things*, it would be more convenient for all men to carry about them such things as were necessary to express the particular business they are to discourse on. And this invention would certainly have taken place, to the great ease as well as health of the subject, if the women, in conjunction with the vulgar and illiterate, had not threatened to raise a rebellion, unless they might be allowed the liberty to speak with their tongues, after the manner of their ancestors; such constant irreconcilable enemies to science are the common people. However, many of the most learned and wise adhere to the new scheme of expressing themselves by things, which hath only this inconvenience attending it, that if a man's business be very great, and of various kinds, he must be obliged in proportion to carry a greater bundle of things upon his back, unless he can afford one or two strong servants to attend him. I have often beheld two of those sages almost sinking under the weight of their packs, like pedlars among us; who, when they meet in the streets, would lay down their loads, open their sacks, and hold conversation for an hour together; then put up their implements, help each other to resume their burthens, and take their leave.
>
> But for short conversations a man may carry implements in his pockets and under his arms, enough to supply him, and in his house he cannot be at a loss. Therefore the room where company meet who practise this art, is full of all things ready at hand, requisite to furnish matter for this kind of artificial converse.
>
> Another great advantage proposed by this invention was that it would serve as an universal language to be understood in all civilised nations, whose goods and utensils are generally of the same kind, or nearly resembling, so that their uses might easily be comprehended. And thus ambassadors would be qualified to treat with foreign princes or ministers of state, to whose tongues they were utter strangers.

To Jonathan Swift, a master of English, there was nothing more golden, more universal, than his own tongue. What the world is actually producing now is more like a multicoloured labyrinth than a golden sphere - more confrontations and translations of languages, more nation-states emerging and having to make linguistic decisions, more interest in minority languages, more languages subdividing (we speak now not of English but of Englishes, a loose federation of diverging forms). And a dialect can become a language. As Max Weinreich said, 'A language is a dialect that has an army and navy.' English itself, now a world languages, was once merely the East Midland dialect of Anglo-Saxon. The vision of one world, with the concomitant vision of one language, will never disappear, but in practice the last fifty or sixty years have seen just as much interest taken in language difference as in the search for a universal grammar, and the tension or dialectic between the two approaches seems to me to be healthy and productive.

Language study in the past was dominantly Indo-European, but when expert linguists began to examine non-Indo-European languages like Chinese and Japanese, or African languages or American Indian languages, they found they were unearthing some very difficult questions about how the world is perceived through language. Physically, it was one world: everyone saw the sun come up, drank water, bled if cut. But beyond that, it began to seem as if there were many worlds. The double fact, first that there are about 4,000 different languages, using what is after all a limited number of sounds (even including clicks and pops), and second that we now know there are no so-called primitive languages, all languages being complex and sophisticated in their own way, really defies speculation. The only analogy in nature is that nature, for its own mysterious purposes, does seem to enjoy a proliferation of forms, perhaps because the clash of differences offers the greatest potential for change and for evolution. In the same way, it may be that the different kinds of social organisation, the different perceptions of the world that are shown through different languages are also a strange, half-understood evolutionary tool which we are just beginning to recognise.

The American linguist Benjamin Lee Whorf (1897-1941) argued for a sort of Einsteinian relativity: that there were as many universes as there were languages. "We are thus introduced", he wrote, "to a new principle of relativity, which holds that all observers are not led by the same physical evidence to the same picture of the universe, unless their linguistic backgrounds are similar, or can in some way be calibrated." Whorf claimed to have discovered, from his study of American Indian languages like Hopi and Aztec, that the structure of these languages, how you expressed yourself in them, was so fundamentally different from Indo-European structures that the underlying structures of thought and perception must also be different. Not everyone believed Whorf, because he seemed to be saying that there was really, when you got down to it, no common universal human experience of the world. But equally, it was clear that there must be *some* truth in what he said, as most translators would testify. The American poet Jerome Rothenberg has made translations of Navajo poetry which bear this out. Here is a passage from his version of 'The Eleventh Horse-Song' of Frank Mitchell (A Navajo Indian, despite his name, who died in 1967). The hero of the poem is a sort of Navajo Prometheus who goes to the house of his father, the Sun, to obtain goods and gifts for the people on Earth, especially horses which became so important in Indian life:

> With my spirit horses that rur white & dawn & holy then some
>   are holy ones N wnn nahht nnn N gahn
> with my spirit howanorses that rur whiteshell & R holy some
>   were holy ones N wnn N nnnn naht gahn
> with my horses that hrr whiteshell & rholy & some were holy
>   ones nahht wnn N nnnn N gahn
> with jewels of evree(ee)ee kind to draw (nn nn) them on & holy
>   & some are holy ones nahht wnn N nnnn N gahn
> with cloth of evree(ee)ee kind to draw (nn nn) them on & holy
>   & some are holy ones nahht wnn N nnnn N gahn
> with sheep of evree(ee)ee kind to draw (nn nn) them on & holy
>   & some are holy ones nahht wnn N nnnn N gahn
> with horses of evree(ee)ee kind to draw (nn nn) them on & holy
>   & some are holy ones nahht wnn N nnnn N gahn
> with cattle of evree(ee)ee kind to draw (nn nn) them on & to be
>   holy & some are holy ones naht wnn N nnnn N gahn
> with men of evree(ee)ee kind to lead N draw (nn nn) them on &
>   holy & some are holy ones nahht wnn N nnnn N gahn
> from my youse of precious jewels to her backackeroom & being
>   holy some were holy ones nahht wnn N nnnn N gahn
> in her house of precious jewels we walk (p)pon & being holy
>   some were holy ones naht wnn N nnnn N gahn
> vvvevrything that's gone beffore M more we walk (f)fon & being
>   holy some were holy ones nahht wnn N nnnn N gahn
> & everything that's more & won't be(be!)be poor & wholly gone &
>   some are holy ones nahht wnn N nnnn N gahn
> & efreedthing that's living to be old (b)b(b)blesst & holy &
>   some are holy ones nahht wnn N nnnn N gahn
> because I am thm boy who blesses/blisses to be old N gahn N
>   holy & some are holy ones nahht wnn N nnnn N gahn
>
> Some are holy ones N wnn & some are holy & some are ones nahht
>   wnn N nnnn N gahn . . .

(From *Open Poetry*, ed. Ronald Gross & George Quasha, NY 1973)

Jerome Rothenberg said that in translating he wanted to show how different Navajo poetry was, but he added that the act of translation made him question and extend his own language, and so confrontations like this, between totally unconnected languages, may help to produce not a world language but something nearer a whole picture of the extraordinary web or maze of the world's languages.

Every language, naturally, wants to defend itself, particularly if it is a language from a stateless nation, or of a newly-liberated nation-state. Strong feelings are involved. When a language is making great efforts to renew itself after a period of either suppression or decline, this may prove alarming to its neighbours, as with Mongolian at the present time. A newspaper despatch from Ulan Bator said the other day: "the crowd erupted into howls of delight at the mention of Genghis Khan, the potent symbol of resurgent Mongolian nationalism." In Scotland, we don't have any figure quite as frightening as that, but we do have our own untidy, nagging language problem, between English, Scots and Gaelic. As soon as someone tries to cut the Gordian knot, like Edwin Muir saying we must drop Scots and use English, we find that ten or twenty years later all three tongues are still wagging and refusing to die out. Iain Crichton Smith, who writes in both English and Gaelic - Gaelic being his mother tongue - has a remarkable poem which speaks for minority languages everywhere, but not in a sentimental spirit, rather by widening the whole issue philosophically. I don't know whether he knows about the Whorfian hypothesis I was describing, but his ideas are very much in line with that. The poem is called 'Shall Gaelic Die?' Here is part of it, translated by the author from his Gaelic original:

Advertisements in neon, lighting and going out, 'Shall it . . . shall it . . . shall Gaelic . . . shall it . . . shall Gaelic . . . die?'

. . . He who loses his language loses his world. The Highlander who loses his language loses his world.
The space ship that goes astray among planets loses the world. In an orange world how would you know orange? In a world without evil how would you know good?

. . . Were you ever in a maze? Its language fits your language. Its roads fit the roads in your head . . . Its roads reflect your language . . .

A million colours are better than one colour, if they are different. A million men are better than one man if they are different . . .

Like a rainbow, like crayons, spectrum of beautiful languages. The one-language descended like a church - like a blanket, like mist.

God is outside language, standing on a perch. He crows now and again. Who hears him? If there is a God let him emanate from the language, a perfume emanating from the dew of the morning, from the various-coloured flowers . . .

The gold is new. It will not rust. 'Immutable universal,' as the Frenchman said. But the pennies, the pounds, the half-crowns, these coins that are old and dirty, the notes that are wrinkled like old faces, they are coping with time; to these I give my allegiance, to these I owe honour, the sweetness. 'Immutable, perfect,' Midas with his coat of gold and of death.

The interest here is not simply that "He who loses his language loses his world", but that the world's languages are praised for their numerousness, their difference, and (most importantly) their imperfection. A million colours, a rainbow, a box of crayons, a spectrum, a fragrant bank of flowers, a maze of winding paths - these are the images he uses. All this multiplicity, this prodigality is contrasted to the idea of 'one-language', dead like a blanket of mist, or worst of all, to the idea of no language, a state of mind so perfect it doesn't need language. Instead of the gold of perfection, it's old worn coins and wrinkled notes he gives his blessing to.

This brings me back, by what Joyce would call "a commodius vicus of recirculation", to my opening point about the moon landings, and my suggestion that the mixture of American and Russian linguistic litter on the moon's surface might be no bad thing. Crichton Smith would not vote for some golden language, some United Nations singlespeak, to replace the clashing Roman and Cyrillic visiting-cards. Working together, speaking, writing together, we do all these things, if we can, not so much by dancing in a ring but by dancing through the maze. Even President Gorbachov has to learn, painfully, how to dance the maze; the circle of empire is breaking, the satellites are escaping. If the 1990s are going to be the age of the periphery, Scotland too may take the plunge; not before time.

Michael Ignatieff, the TV commentator and philosopher, has said recently: "I think all attachments are elective. People think attachments have to be attachments of birth, attachments of fate." I'm sure he says this because of his own mixed background, Russian-Scottish-Canadian. But some writers would certainly agree with him. Joseph Conrad made himself into an English novelist. Samuel Beckett wrote plays in flawless French. Kafka wrote stories in German, not Czech. The theologian St Francis Xavier and the philosopher Unamuno were both Basques, but wrote in Spanish, which was fine for them but didn't help the Basques. There are always two ways of looking at such examples. Everyone who writes writes for everyone. You write as a human being, and you hope your work will be read and enjoyed, someday, in countries other than your own.

And yet we also have deep feelings about nation and language; few writers don't, when you probe them. Kafka came to feel guilty about losing his Czech inheritance; no one, even in France, would think of Beckett as other than an Irish writer; and there are books on Conrad as a Polish novelist. It's a dilemma that has no solution, but it is important to acknowledge that it *is* a dilemma. If you asked St Francis Xavier why he used Spanish, he would say, 'For communication! I must use one of the world languages!' But, in answer to that defence, you cannot but regret that the great Basques of history - and there are quite a few - had to jettison their own language, the oldest tongue in Europe. However, I feel that the old assumption, the lazy assumption that minority languages would continue to decline and eventually vanish, and that this was not a matter of huge concern, has changed, and that the climate now is more favourable and positive. It may be connected with the emergence of so many new nation-states since the last war, or run parallel with conservation ideas about endangered species, or go along with our new scientific understanding of the interest, complexity and expressiveness of minority languages, but whatever the reasons, it does seem to be a good time to start, let us say, learning Albanian?

At any rate, here we are in Glasgow, in this little core on peripheral Scotland, looking outwards as we should do, maybe not to Saturn but to those matters across the world that interest and concern us and bring us together. Whether the coming week will prove to be a ring or a maze, I hope everyone will enjoy it.

Edwin Morgan

Edwin Morgan: photograph by Kevin Low

"An Island In The City..."

Edwin Morgan's Urban Poetry

Roderick Watson

The poet in the city

It was William Wordsworth, in 1805, who first identified what the city would come to mean to so many writers in our time: (*The Prelude*, Book VII)

> How often in the overflowing streets
> Have I gone forwards with the crowd, and said
> Unto myself, "The face of every one
> That passes by me is a mystery!" . . .
> And once . . .   . . . lost
> Amid the moving pageant, 'twas my chance
> Abruptly to be smitten with the view
> Of a blind Beggar who, with upright face,
> Stood propped against a wall, upon his chest
> Wearing a written paper, to explain
> The story of the man, and who he was.
> My mind did at this spectacle turn round
> As with the might of waters - and it seemed
> To me that in this label was a type,
> or emblem of the utmost that we know
> Both of ourselves and of the universe;
> And on the shape of the unmoving man,
> His fixed face and sightless eyes, I looked
> As if admonished from another world.

At sea in a sea of other faces, the blind beggar speaks for the enigma of individual experience and, despite a placard with his 'story' on it, he also stands for the incommunicable nature of suffering. Faced with such a sight, Wordsworth might well have cried, as Edwin Morgan does when remembering a blind hunchback in a snack-bar: "Dear Christ, to be born for this!". Other people and inner solitary darkness are the themes of this essay.

Wordsworth developed his vision of the city by going on to describe the carnival at Smithfield Market, on St Bartholomew's day every August:

> . . . What a hell
> For eyes and ears! what anarchy and din
> Barbarian and infernal - 'tis a dream
> Monstrous in colour, motion, shape, sight, sound!
> Below, the open space, through every nook
> Of the wide area, twinkles, is alive
> With heads; the midway region and above
> Is thronged with staring pictures, and huge scrolls,
> Dumb proclamations of the Prodigies; . . .
> The Wax-work, Clock-work, all the marvellous craft

Of modern Merlins, Wild Beasts, Puppet-shows,
All out-o'the-way, far-fetched, perverted things,
All freaks of Nature, all Promethian thoughts
Of man; his dullness, madness, and their feats
All jumbled up together, to make up
This Parliament of Monsters. Tents and Booths,
Meanwhile, as if the whole were one vast mill,
Are vomiting, receiving, on all sides,
Men, Women, three-years' Children, Babes in arms.
   Oh blank confusion! and a type not false
Of what the mighty City is itself
To all except a straggler here and there,
To the whole swarm of its inhabitants; . . .
Living amid the same perpetual flow
Of trivial objects, melted and reduced
To one identity, by differences
That have no law, no meaning, and no end -

Here the sensory bombardment of the city streets, and the loneliness of the crowds who walk them, have gone beyond the representation of a particular urban scene, to become symbols of what will soon be thought of as 'modern' existence in general. Indeed, the nature of our present century is well summed-up by those "Promethian thoughts" amid the "perpetual flow of trivial objects", and the same combination can be found in many of Edwin Morgan's poems in *The Second Life*, or *From Glasgow to Saturn*.

Baudelaire's poem 'Le Cygne' offers a similar vision from 1860, as the poet wanders the streets and comes across an escaped swan, trailing its magnificent white plumage in the gutter, gasping in vain for water amid the dust and the noise of the roadmenders. Here among the changing streets of Paris "everything becomes an allegory" for the poet, and Baudelaire looks around the new palaces, the scaffolding, the blocks of building-stone and the old suburbs, to think of those who live there like people who have been captive or defeated, or like "sailors forgotten on a desert island".

Such images are more than familiar to readers on the other side of Eliot's waste land, and in modern literature the city has been a powerful, and usually a pessimistic, motif. In this context the roots of modernism can be traced through Dickens to Dostoevsky and Thomson's *City of Dreadful Night*, not to mention W E Henley's Hospital poems ("Life is, I think, a blunder and a shame"), and John Davidson's 'The Crystal Palace', which is itself so very like Wordsworth's original vision of St Bartholomew's fair.

Edwin Morgan's city poems have a distinguished place in this line of descent, and he acknowledges an early debt to Baudelaire, Eliot and Thomson ('Nothing is not giving messages' in *Nothing Not Giving Messages*, Polygon 1990). But Morgan has been less pessimistic than his precursors by tending to welcome change and new technology in areas where many British poets have found only alienation and despair. In this respect he has more in common with poets such as Walt Whitman, Carl Sandburg and Hart Crane. Indeed, Morgan has written an essay on Crane's great poem *The Bridge*, which recognises its celebration of the energy and bustle of the urban masses (and Brooklyn Bridge itself) as symbols of mobility, communication and creativity in a new world. Morgan's essential optimism is best summed up in 'The Second Life', the title poem of the 1968 collection which marked his arrival on the scene as a mature poet of real power and significance.

But does every man feel like this at forty -
I mean it's like Thomas Wolfe's New York, his
heady light, the stunning plunging canyons, beauty -
pale stars winking hazy-downtown-quitting-time,
and the winter moon flooding the skyscrapers, northern -
an aspiring place, glory of the bridges, foghorns
are enormous messages . . .
Can it be like this, and is this what it means
in Glasgow now, writing as the aircraft roar
over building sites, in the warm west light
by the daffodil banks that were never so crowded and lavish -
green May, and the slow great blocks rising
under yellow tower cranes, concrete and glass and steel
out of dour rubble it was and barefoot children gone -

- Here Wordsworth's daffodils and Baudelaire's building sites rub shoulders with "yellow tower cranes", and Morgan can find the capacity for wonder and delight in them all.

This vision of a "second life" stemmed from Glasgow's urban renewal of the mid-60s, and Morgan has since recognised (with the ironies of hindsight) that that renewal was not without its own destructive costs. We know more now about the alienation of high-rise tower-blocks, and the cost of motorways in place of (or on top of) once-lived-in streets. Yet there was that determination to grow and to change, however late in the city's economic life it might have seemed, to be making a new start. And, at the age of 40, 'The Second Life' speaks of the poet's own determination to recognise his own special nature and to change and to grow as well:

Many things are unspoken
in the life of a man, and with a place
there is an unspoken love also
in undercurrents, drifting, waiting its time.
A great place and its people are not renewed lightly.
The caked layers of grime
grow warm, like homely coats.
But yet they will be dislodged
and men will still be warm.
The old coats are discarded.
The old ice is loosed.
The old seeds are awake.

A similar determination to salute the new marked many of Morgan's Glasgow poems from the collections of the 60s and 70s, and his city streets can offer a constant source of novelty and optimism. In 'Trio', for example, even "fate" is vanquished and the "vale of tears" is found to be "powerless" in the face of no more than a young man and two girls out shopping on

Buchanan Street. This is not a conventional Christmas poem, for Morgan's "march of three" (with baby in shawl, chihuahua in tartan coat and guitar in plastic cover), will triumph "whether Christ is born, or is not born". The same "flow of trivial objects" is given a glorious drunken energy in 'Saturday Night', a poem written in one long sentence; and then there's the cheerful destruction of old things, old news and old pains celebrated in the three poems called 'For Bonfires'. First garden rubbish, then crumbling slums, and finally old letters are cheerfully sent on their way: "The black pages fuse/ to a single whispering mass/ threaded by dying tracks of gold./ Let them grow cold,/ and when they're dead/ quickly draw breath. ('For Bonfires iii').

There's equal celebration in the long poem 'London' in which the old terraces, the parks, the Rabelaisian surrealism of Soho, and the aerials and satellite dishes on the Post Office Tower are all joined together in a new kind of urban pastoral, given over only to the immediate present moment:

> There is no other life,
> and this is it.
> Gold bars, thunder, gravity, wine, concrete, smoke.
> And the blue pigeon London sky
> hangs high heat on towers, a summer shower
> on trees, its clouds
> to swing over cranes
> that swing slowly
> blue vaguely.
> We are drawn to the welder's star.
> Ships we half see.
> Glass walls flash new cliffsides, brick-beds
> brood with dust, red, gray, grey, blue.
> Huge shadows skim the classic terraces.
> Hunt sun hunt cloud, one long morning.

This is far from Wordsworth's "blank confusion", with "no law, no meaning, and no end." Nor does Morgan have to a higher presence to support his good faith, for the poem begins "There is no other life". If he follows a star at all, he is drawn to the spark of a welder's torch. As with 'Trio', the poet can find redemption in these streets, "whether Christ is born or is not born."

But this is not the only face the city shows to Morgan. There are the 'Glasgow Sonnets' in which that "shilpit dog fucks grimly by the close"; and grimmer, blanker poems such as 'Death in Duke Street' with "an auld fella, he's had it . . ." and its closing lines: "Only the hungry ambulance/ howls for him through the staring squares." In 'Stobhill' a number of witnesses and protagonists tell how an aborted foetus in the Stobhill Hospital boiler room was found to be still (just) living on its way to the incinerator. The doctor, the boilerman, the parents and the porter all tell their stories and make their excuses in a poem which has the relentless light of a neon tube over a bench in a clinical laboratory. The same painstaking documentary impulse - detailed, precise and almost successfully deadpan in its utterance - can be found in the widely-anthologised poem, 'In the Snack-bar'.

'Glasgow Sonnets', 'Death in Duke Street', 'Stobhill', 'In the Snack-bar' and other poems all show that Morgan has faced the nightmare too, and shared something of Wordsworth's vision of a modern city as a Bartholomew's Fair - a "Parliament of Monsters . . . jumbled up together". And yet he has also enjoyed and celebrated the glittering surface of the contemporary urban world, and (more than any other poet writing in English today) he has welcomed the products of modern technology and made them part of his art. These two points of view mark the opposite poles of his engagement with the city, and can be found side by side in collections of his poems. I want to examine this confrontation, and what Morgan makes of it at a personal level. There is tenderness in his best city poems, and yet a lonely darkness, too. In the last analysis I believe that Morgan is still a creative optimist, but it can be difficult for us (and sometimes, I think, for him too), to bring the precise grounds for that optimism into the light.

The city in the poet:

Some of Morgan's most memorable despatches from the city can be found in the 'Instamatic' poems which he began to write in the early 70s, beginning with the collection called *Instamatic Poems* from 1972. These take the form of imagined 'snapshots' of actual events reported in the press. In the global village of the modern news media we learn to distance ourselves from the stories of pain and human suffering which assail us at every turn. And yet we remain indecently intimate with such images, at least for the moment before we change channels or turn to the next page of news. (Wordsworth's blind man no longer tells his 'story' with a piece of paper round his neck - his plight is broadcast to thousands every day.)

There are witty and entertaining Instamatic poems, but the majority are grim. Morgan aims for a documentary detachment, along the lines of "I am a camera", but the cumulative result of reading a number of them is less like objectivity and more like a kind of moral blankness. First we are shocked, then there is a frisson of morbid interest, and then we turn away. This is the essence of human experience daily in our crowded cities. It's how we sustain our privacy, and also, perhaps, personal security. And yet Morgan will not let us turn away, or at least he will show ourselves to ourselves as we do it:

> With a ragged diamond
> of shattered plate-glass
> a young man and his girl
> are falling backwards into a shop-window.
> The young man's face
> is bristling with fragments of glass
> and the girl's leg has caught
> on the broken window
> and spurts arterial blood
> over her wet-look white coat.
> Their arms are starfished out
> braced for impact,
> their faces show surprise, shock,
> and the beginning of pain.
> The two youths who have pushed them

> are about to complete the operation
> reaching into the window
> to loot what they can smartly.
> Their faces show no expression.
> It is a sharp clear night
> in Sauchiehall Street.
> In the background two drivers
> keep their eyes on the road.

('Glasgow 5 March 1971') Like many of the Instamatic pieces, this poem also registers a vicarious and morbid fascination with such events present in the poet (consciously or otherwise) just as it is present in ourselves.

In another essay, (in *Insights into British Poetry in the 20th Century*, Macmillan 1991), I have discussed how a number of these poems are still in fact transformed by metaphor and symbol, as if Morgan's art couldn't help but assert itself in the face of such events. There is no such thing as a neutral photograph, after all, and so it is likely that the writer will betray conscious and unconscious feelings through his choice of vocabulary or subject matter. The above example is not much transformed, but it is still telling us more than the facts alone would suggest. There is a horrid aestheticism at work in the juxtaposition of arterial blood on a white "wet-look" coat; and there is a cluster of ironic puns to be found in the conflation of "*starfish*" with a ragged "diamond" of plate glass, in that "*sharp* clear night". These lexical links hint at a larger and stranger metaphor which has something to do with living in the depths, and the sudden confrontation with the jewel-like sharpness (and value?) of a violent and ultimately existential awareness ("the beginning of pain"). Then again, the "surprised" looks of the boy and his girl contrast with the "expressionless" faces of the two youths, and the carefully blank faces of the two drivers, for whom keeping their "eyes on the road" is a more than usual guarantee of personal safety.

It is the *blankness* of those eyes, like the blankness of the encounter itself, which speaks most powerfully of how Morgan sees the darker side of urban experience, and yet there's a strangely disturbing richness here, too - at least from an artistic point of view. It has to do, I think, with an odd sense the poet frequently has of people not present, connections not made, and things unsaid or unsayable. Morgan's vision of what it's like to live in the middle of Bartholomew's Fair is at its most poignant at such moments, taking us back to Baudelaire's vision of the city as a crowded but lonely dream: *"Je pense aux matelots oubliés dans un île/ Aux captifs, aux vaincus!"*

Absence of a literal sort is at the heart of another Instamatic poem: 'Glasgow November 1971', which might well be the darker side of 'Trio' in which the "monsters of the year" *don't* "go blank", or perhaps their "blankness" wins, for once, in the Christmas crowded streets.

> It is a fine thronged Christmas shopping afternoon
> in Argyll street . . .
> The evening shadows
> cannot be far away. The Royston boy
> of thirteen murdered by the Blackhill boy

of twelve is gone. The stolen ring
they scuffled for is gone. The stolen kitchen knife
that sank into his side is gone.
The big store writes off knife and ring, but someone
has set out pail and broom
convenient on the pavement.
They wait in the foreground, sturdy objects,
the iron pail with its handle up,
the long broom carefully balanced on the handle,
and the dark spread of blood between them.

Those "evening shadows" which "cannot be far away" are the very same shadows that haunt the poem 'Glasgow Green'. In that poem they are the shadows of violence; or perhaps of homosexual assignation; or of gang rape. They are the anonymous shapes of "meth men muttering on benches." ". . . All shadows are alive/ somewhere a shout's forced out - No! -/ it leads to nothing but silence,/ except the whisper of the grass/ and the other whispers that fill the shadows./ "What d'ye mean see me again?/ D'ye think I came here jist for that?/ I'm no finished with you yet. I can get the boys t'ye, they're no that faur away." The poem claims a place for such "alive" shadows, ("do you think there is not a seed of the thorn/ as there is also a harvest of the thorn?") and ends with a vision that conventional bourgeois life (the "beds of married love") is merely an island in a tenebrous "sea of desire": "Its waves break here, in this park,/ splashing the flesh as it trembles/ like driftwood through the dark."

Morgan evokes the shadow-world of human life on the streets with power and compassion. Although his sense of the vulnerabliity of these outsiders may stem from his own sexuality (see 'Power from things not declared' in *Nothing Not Giving Messages*, Polygon 1990), his words speak to the common experience of anyone who has lived alone or travelled alone through any city. His poem 'Christmas Eve' makes this sense of solitary precariousness quite explicit, and it's no coincidence that it's another 'Christmas' piece, when the lone traveller must confront cheerful crowds of people who are dedicated to what is essentially a family festival.

I sat down on the bus beside him - white jeans
black jerkin, slumped with head nodding
in sleep, face hidden by long black hair, hands
tattooed on the four fingers ADEN 1967
and on the right hand five Christian crosses.
As the bus jerked, his hand fell on my knee,
stayed there, lay heavily and alive
with blue carvings from another world
and seemed to hold me like a claw,
unmoving. It moved. I rubbed my ear
to steal a glance at him, found him
stealing a glance at me. It was not
the jerking of the bus, it was a proposition.
He shook his hair back, and I saw his face

for the first time, unshaven, hardman, a warning
whether in Aden òr Glasgow, but our eyes held
While that blue hand burned into my leg.
Half drunk, half sleeping - but half what, half what?
As his hand stirred again, my arm covered it
while the bus jolted round a corner.
"Don't ge' aff tae ah ge' aff." - But the conductor
was watching, came up and shook him, looked at me.
My ticket was up. I had to leave him sprawled there
with that hand that now seemed so defenceless
lying on the seat I had left. Half down the stair
I looked back. The last thing I saw was Aden
and five blue crosses for five dead friends.

It was only fifteen minutes out of life
but I feel as if I was lifted by a whirlwind
and thrown down on some desert rocks to die
of dangers as always far worse lost than run.

Those "blue carvings from another world" are just as evocative for Morgan as Wordsworth's encounter with the blind beggar had been ("I looked, as if admonished from another world"). But in Morgan's poetry they lead us back to the shadows of 'Glasgow Green' and the plea that "the race shall be served" by "anguish" and "loneliness", as well as by "children at play", or "family love", or "those who turn back the sheets in peace."

Wordsworth observed anguish and loneliness in the noisy carnival of the city, but Morgan reminds us that these feelings are also part of human love: homosexual or heterosexual, it makes no difference. In this respect the city can echo a creative darkness within us all, and this is not just the darkness of total isolation and despair. There are dangers, in our daily encounters with each other - dangers of *not* turning away - that are better "run" than "lost".

Some of Morgan's finest love poems take the city as their setting for just this reason, I think. The city is the ideal *topos* through which to convey his sense of the vulnerability of the human condition, trembling "like driftwood through the dark", in poems of great tenderness and yet poignant isolation. This is a side to his inspiration most markedly different from his more familiar and more playful poems in praise of modernity and all its ingenious gadgets. There are many fine love poems which could be cited, but 'Absence', from *The Second Life*, is particularly notable for its imagery (once again) of the shadow.

Our shadow is that which is intimate to us, we cannot separate from it, and yet it is a no-thing. It is also a familiar symbol of the other self, a secret sharer perhaps, half what we seem to be, and yet also ". . . half what, half what?" The poem introduces the image of fire, (perhaps for passion) and yet it is only a dreamed fire when all is said and done, and the poem ends instead with images of the wind - something else in our experience which is familiar and omnipresent, but intangible. Or to be more accurate, tangible, but uncatchable. The wind is a long-established symbol of the soul and inspiration, but it is also an epigram for futility.

My shadow -
I woke to a wind swirling the curtains light and dark
and the birds twittering on the roofs, I lay cold
in the early light in my room high over London.
What fear was it that made the wind sound like a fire
so that I got up and looked out half-asleep
at the calm rows of street-lights fading far below?
Without fire only the wind blew.
But in the dream .I woke from, you
came running through the traffic, tugging me, clinging
to my elbow, your eyes spoke
what I could not grasp -
Nothing, if you were here!

The wind of the early quiet
merges slowly now with a thousand rolling wheels.
The lights are out, the air is loud.
It is an ordinary January day.
My shadow, do you hear the streets?
Are you at my heels? Are you there?
And I throw back the sheets.   ('Absence')

This is not the city of Eliot's *Preludes* - a grim place of damp and sprouting despair. Morgan's poems confront larger, healthier mysteries, though no less dark, perhaps. There is a poignant sense of absence, but not of loss or defeat. At the end of the first section the poem uses a syntactical elusiveness (about "absence") to invoke the sheer joy of "presence" in the eyes of a loved one - and all beyond words. That is to say, the poet proposes that eyes can "speak" what cannot be "grasped"; there is "nothing" that he cannot grasp when his lover is present: everything is within his reach.

We can read these lines in another, and darker way. In this reading, the lover's eyes are simply incomprehensible (what they say cannot be grasped), and even if the loved one *were* present, all that we ultimately hold on such occasions is "nothing". This second reading is submerged within the first, and secondary to it, but it still represents a wider, colder truth, *sub specie aeternitatis* as it were, and far beyond the immediate thrill of mere human affections. Having said that, the last rhyme "streets/sheets" links the private world of the lovers (or rather the dreamer and the dreamed), with the workaday social world outside, in what seems to me to be a positive way.

'Dear Man, My Love Goes Out in Waves', a particularly fine poem written in 1987 and published in *Themes on a Variation*, nearly 20 years after 'Absence', brings these themes together in a bleaker mood, evoking personal feeling, absence and the vulnerable individual in the city. Contradiction and insecurity alternate with a tentative confidence in love, and although it's a personal lyric, it engages with a larger perspective on existence, summed up in a grim and stirring line: "Whatever is, craves". The poem returns to those images of waves and darkness first established in 'Glasgow Green' as metaphors of the all-too-mortal human flesh. These images revolve around the vision that we long for contact among the crowds of life, and yet we also fear contact. And contact may never be possible anyway. Even the syntax and the line-breaks of the poem act out this central paradox:

> Dear man, my love goes out in waves
> and breaks. Whatever is, craves.
> Terrible the cage
> to see all life from, brilliantly about,
> crowds, pavements, cars, or hear the common shout
> of goals in a near park.
> But now the black bars arc
> blue in my breath - split - part -
> I'm out - it's art,
> it's love, it's rage -
>
> Standing in rage in decent air
> will never clear the place of care.
> Simply to be
> should be enough, in the same city, and let
> absurd despair tramp and roar off-set.
> Be satisfied with it,
> the gravel and the grit
> the struggling eye can't lift,
> the veils that drift,
> the weird to dree.
>
> Press close to me at midnight as
> you say goodbye; that's what it has
> to offer, life
> I mean. Into the frost with you; into
> the bed with me; and get the light out too.
> Better to shake unseen
> and let real darkness screen
> the shadows of the heart,
> the vacant part-
> ner, husband, wife.

The heart of this poem lies in the different ways it engages with the word "break". Waves break when they arrive on the shore to consummate the end of their journey. But love breaks (fractures) when fulfilment cannot be found. The first two lines play with both possibilities. Then the poet speaks of breaking out of the cage around us, and how we can split the bars that keep us alone by speaking strongly through love, rage or art. But that is not enough: we still need love or companionship, even if it is simply being in the same city as the loved one. The final stanza involves a different kind of break at midnight, as the poet parts from his lover, who must return to some other life, leaving the speaker in a lonely bed. In the last analysis what "life" has to offer is no more than a close embrace as we say goodbye, and so "Into the frost with you" and "get the light out too" might have a harder, darker and more bitterly dismissive tone to them than is first apparent.

From these roots the poem explores a terrible tension between the urge towards contact, and the urge to avoid it, and the syntactical structure and the line-breaks themselves echo this confusion, particularly over what "it" might be in each stanza. In the first stanza "it" might refer to "art", "love" or "rage"; to the poet's declaration of love in the first place ("I'm out"), or even to the poem itself as it's happening on the page. "Be satisfied with it" in the second stanza is equally problematical. The primary and most optimistic reading would refer to the claim that "Simply to be/ should be enough". But "it" could also refer to "absurd despair" always ready to make a noise in the wings; or to the "gravel and the grit" of city life, those everyday irritants and veils that blind us to our fate. In the final stanza "it" can be taken to mean "life", as indeed the poet assures us it does ("life/ I mean"). But the other reading, and the one he has tried to suppress, is that such "goodbyes" are what "midnight" has to offer, and the associations brought to mind by "midnight" are altogether darker than those conjured up by "life".

If these readings seem to cast more darkness than light on the subject, that is the point of the poem. Morgan has evolved a spiky, ambiguous grammar, and those oddly broken line endings, to express the tensions of commitment and evasion raging within the poem. This is never more clear than in the closing lines. "Better to shake unseen/ and let real darkness screen/ the shadows of the heart,/ the vacant part-/ ner, husband, wife."

The poem ends by concluding that it's better to hide the violent and vulnerable shadows within us in "real darkness". And what we find within us is no more than "the vacant part". But then we notice that the line is somehow truncated ("part-" rather than "part"), and its interruption encourages us to read it as it stands, a phrase cut off in mid-sentence, perhaps, something started then abandoned. Of course the wider context soon reveals to us that it is a complete word, "partner", which has been interrupted, and indeed it is around this signifier that the emotional tensions and the structural tensions of the whole poem have been enlisted at the most acute level.

'Dear man . . .' revolves around the need for and the absence or ultimate loss of a partner. Or perhaps the "vacant partner" is the waiting "husband" or the wronged "wife" of the lover who has just left the poet's bed at midnight. In either case "vacant" is an astonishing and terrible substitution for what the literal logic of the line might require, which I take to be 'absent' as in "absent partner". Those last two lines simultaneously evoke the "vacant part" of the human heart; then either the poet's absent partner or his lover's; and finally the ultimately existential "vacancy" which lies at the heart of all our encounters with each other. ("Press close to me . . . as/ you say goodbye: that's what it has/ to offer, life/ I mean.")

Opening with a fragmented and scarcely-stressed syllable, the last line undermines any confidence that there might be stability or reliability to be found in the roles of "husband" or "wife". They are overshadowed by that preceding fragment, for "the vacant part-" is evocative of Morgan's specially lonely sense of what life in the city is like, and how city experience can become a central metaphor for human encounters. The "vacant part" is that which we long somehow to fill, and we all carry something of it within the streets and squares of ourselves: "Terrible the cage/ to see all life from,/ brilliantly about,/ crowds, pavements, cars, or hear the common shout/ of goals in a near park."

Roderick Watson

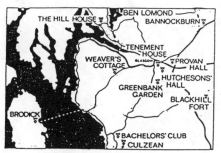

Edwin Morgan

A FUCHSIA

I rescued it three years ago from rubbish.
Half-dead, a limp ungainly arc of ripped-off
green, it lay without a flower to recommend it
and somehow like a spring or snake it challenged
the logic of the vertical, resisted
potting; but I firmed it, staked it, waited.
Sometimes it's barish, sometimes bushy; tries, though.
This summer it decided to be bushy,
parachutes pushed out, dangling pink and purple,
trembling as container lorries rumbled,
almost nodding to make me say I loved them,
and so I do, you hear that, you strange plant you,
it's true. You don't love me but I sense something -
no I can't be mistaken, it's next to palpable -
you're bent, a down-turned cup-hook, and without propping
you would collapse into the earth you came from,
so why should you keep flowering so gamely -
I can't but think it speaks to me, your living
loaded curve of grace steadily bearing,
but the best bearing, the best blooming, is moral,
or if that cannot be - who am I to say so,
is chlorophyll so dumb - at least I'm sending,
like an antenna - don't shake, I don't mean insects -
waves of encouragement, solidarities of
struggle, gratitude even for imaginary
gratitude, though who knows what a fuchsia
feels, plucked from dump and dust, from a gehenna
to this west kitchen window, rays of evening
and more mysterious light of human glances.

A VISIT

There's another. That's another. And another.
They seem to come to us from their own country
as if they loved us, or found something sustaining
in roofs and woods, airs of blue and pavements,
waters still and wild. Whether they have nothing,
or have become tired of whatever brilliance
it was they swooped from, or are merely knocking
by chance on this world's half-hinged storm-door
because they saw a gleam inside that teased them,
or heard some engine-puttering that pleased them,

Illustration to 'Fuchsia' by Gillian Ferguson

there's nothing in our universe to tell us.
If you want help, you must undo your secrets!
If you attack us, we shall not be gentle!
And yet you seem to come and go uncaring,
strangers to solicitation, travelling
who knows what endless circuits that must break here
as briefly to you as we might watch a paper
we cannot read caught on some swirling freeway
before it gusts off white through wastelands into
air and vanishes 'among the cloud-banks.

A QUESTION

The were so anxious, yet they had some spirit.
Some of them shook their fists at us, though mostly
they plodded, scurried, frowned about their business
as we'd been told they would. What was most striking
was that things did hold, the many intersections
did somehow flow through one another, order
without calm did seem to work, not always -
we saw their blood, and bits - but surely something
had ground together in a great coherence -
they could not see it, but we did, we could see it -
over a few hundred thousand years of using
their planet, well, badly, up, no matter,
we know and they know there are others waiting
for spade and drill and geodesic dome. Well then,
but why is it not that, but this, this only
I cannot relegate, forget, make sense of,
how one of them stood there intently watching -
he was not young, not a fool - a piece of newspaper
caught in traffic, blown then across wastelands,
up among clouds where - and that's all - it vanished?

A COACH-TOUR (J.G.S.)

You did not know it, but nothing you could do to me
was worse than your silence when you were angry.
Often when I did wrong as a boy, my parents
refused the release of storming it out, pretended
I was not there, went on talking to each other,
brushing past me to wash and dry the dishes.
Nothing seemed more terrible, more cruel.
How can I say that, never nagged or beaten
as some are, or thrown out? We have to witness
what was, and those withdrawals, obliterations

planted such deadly fears of being abandoned
that when you made your face go blank and crossed your
legs and never let the jolting coach-tour
bring our bodies into faintest contact
I was cast back into an ancient panic,
sweating in my summer clothes, staring rigid
ahead, though gorgeous trees flashed past the window.
I saw a sole path that led out to ruins.
What did you feel? Ah but I know, exactly.

A MORATORIUM

Let us have no more memories, erase them.
Drive up to the moratorium doors where bouncers
are nailing archivists to hardwood panels.
You will not mention last year's drought, far less the
dinosaurs. 'Only a week ago, I - ' 'Off with his
head.' 'Remember how you used to - ' 'Off with
her head.' 'Once upon a time, children, there were -
'Off with their heads.' The moratorium period
is one year, and in that year no past tenses
will be allowed. I want to see you all living -
and I mean living - you don't burnish the trumpet
you play the trumpet, you don't knot the quipu
you say this is the eighth of June the day of
sacrifices when we give the past its
obsidian. Runners on the altiplano
are up like jaguars. History's jugular
drips. A calendar snatched by a condor
flutters high and higher till the soaring
days dissolve in hungry sunlight. Gullets
of eternal blue - do you hear me - are terrifyingly,
gigantically, beautifully open.

A PARTICULAR COUNTRY

No philosophers darkened that country.
Decreation, deconstruction died there
in the hot loamy burst of seedlings, squabs' teeth
cracking shells in zigzags, rain-forests
torn to shreds by squawks and shrieks that left them
untorn. As for general ideas,
a blowpipe picked them off, they joined the leaf-mould
to mulch minute minuter and minutest
particulars. Watered silk had nothing
on those vibrancies, creakings, thrustings, scatterings,

splash and flicker, drop and web, smudge and whirr, endless
intermitted unpredictable form-crinklings,
rhubarb-clumps with peacocks in a downpour,
what a sparkle of lushnesses, what a catmint
to roll in, what a maze of eyes to thread, that
mass of change and chance and challenge where you
go out; sink in; draw deep at signs that daze you
as stock might, in the nights of your own country.

A FLYPAST

Symphonic shreds had just swept off with Schnittke
when two swans flew like spirits past my window.
Russia, music, soul, said the television,
nature, it said, harmony, ideal.
The long necks stretched, smelt their swan lake, laboured
forward till the trees hid them. And eastern,
the television said, Armenian, Azeri
horizontality, the patterns endless,
keeping western verticals at bay while
voices circle over silent marshes.
Well, I don't know. My startling flyers flapping
so steady and so low over the van-tops,
the hissing wheels, the sirens and the skateboards,
knew where they were going and had shattered
in their rising from some placid water mirror
a harmony too famous, strode the air-streams
to turn how many heads at windows as we
wonder that we ever thought them spirits,
those muscles working, those webs, that eye, that purpose.

AN ATRIUM

At first we loved the plate-glass glare, the car-horns,
the swarthy shoppers and the garrulous market -
I haggled a set of skewers for 'what kebabs would
that be?' you said laughing - but we sauntered
out of the heat at last, through a huge doorway,
into a hall made cool with many fountains,
green with palms like columns, silver-columned
with steel like stylised palms, a floor of marble,
and faint muzak from unseen grilles drifting
among the water-drops to make real music,
Cage-like, as our shoes clacked in. Above us -
we could hardly not look up - seemed endless -
the vast round space retreated to the plainest

of pure blue domes that only its gentle shining
showed as not the sky we thought we wanted.
We were enclosed in a great peace pretending
to infinity; the infinity of thinking
came to us without pretence, with wonder, gladness,
amazed fall of the shell of self to the marble,
diamond awareness of others like coloured jewels
walking, talking, smoking, smiling slowly
or sitting on stone benches with their papers,
watching their children dip a hand in waters
that had left paradise that very midday
and brought it to them, brought it to them. Surely
we too were moved by gifts we'd never chaffered,
the poor brass toys we clutched had become earnests
of something we would never define, not golden,
not silver, not even green, but only
a murmur, a goodness, a gushing spring, an echo.

A BLACK DOG DAY

Pour, pour down, light like water, any acre,
any square or warren, any crossroads
of this habble will do. Drench them with your searches,
flash-flood the sweating truncheons from their dust-clouds,
fall pitilessly on the tear-gassed babies,
wash us with our lies into the syvers.

AT POPPY'S

Karen you know this is *quite* improper.
These eyelashes *were* on my dressing-table.
It's no use telling me you never saw them.
If you're after Monsieur Jack you can forget it,
he likes the natural look. I know you took them,
I'm not accusing you of anything, just
telling you. You're such a slut in waiting.
Fishnets all right, but fishnets with *finesse*, dear.
Hunks have their niceties, they may be shyish -
yes, laugh, it gives you away, that, *raucous* -
I said real men are sensitive to details,
and if you *have* to be an understudy
then you must study. Just because you're younger
you won't be jumping rungs, *that* I can tell you.
Get yourself together, get some nous. Darling
don't *sulk*. A quick pout sometimes can work wonders

but I assure you permanent creases downward
from the mouth are *death*, a lower lip thrusting
upward *death plus one*, so re-lax. Now I've
got my eyes back I can sweep you up and
down and well, if you simply stopped cultivating
those passé sultry slouches you'd have something.
Books, that's it, book on head, walkabout.
What's this old thing, a Trollope, that'll suit you -
I can't read titles, never mind, here take it.
Now let me see you walk. The calves! The shoulders!
Tell your body who's the boss. Do it!
Forward. Round. Mind the table! Back. Smiling!
Don't look as if you'd prunes that hadn't worked yet.
Carriage! That's what we want, like in the old days.
Carriage, my dear, as if you'd melt a ballroom
merely by flowing down the stairs in satin,
at the last step twitching a few lightnings
with one hand as you show a shoe, hide it,
and take the floor. Karen you're not listening!
I keep a good house here. What do they pay for -
sleaze queens? You don't want class you're not for Poppy's.
Pick up the book. Once more. Don't *strut*. Walking!

A FULL MOON

The moon with its old beauty and blank power,
crisscrossed by unseen unchanging bootprints -
take a curler's broom to sweep your tracks back! -
slinks from left to right above the rooftops -
I'm watching it, that's my reluctant tribute
to a mass of rock with light on its deserts -
and vanishes steadily beyond a sight-line
that suddenly seems deprived, left in a blankness
greater than the moon's - crane, strain, the house-wall's
got it, someone else's window's filling,
it's all right! - but the mind, magnetised, misses
the dark man gathering sticks in the story,
the rayed craters of reality, the voyage
of an image soldered into imagination
by the megalith builders and those before them,
and if there were giants on the earth, well then,
they would make their bonfires by its brilliance
and shout at it, wading their stormy foreshore.
I rise and switch the light off like a lift-off.

FIRES

What is that place, my father and my mother,
you have gone to, I think of, in the ashes
of the air and not the earth, better to go there
than under stones or in any remembrance
but mine and that of others who once loved you,
fewer year on year. It is midsummer
and till my voice broke, *Summer suns are glowing*
I loved to sing and *One fine day* to hear from
some thin wild old gramophone that carried
its passion across the Rutherglen street, invisibly
played again and again - I thought of that person,
him or her, as taking me to a country
far high sunny where I knew to be happy
was only a moment, a puttering flame in the fireplace
but burning all the misery to cinders
if it could, a sift of dross like what we mourn for
as caskets sink with horrifying blandness
into a roar, into smoke, into light, into almost nothing.
The not quite nothing I praise it and I write it.

Edwin Morgan

Morgan's Critical Position

Robert Crawford

Morgan's prose is the most provocative assembly of literary criticism to be produced by a later-20th century Scottish creative writer. His 1974 volume of *Essays* is all the stronger for its consideration of foreign as well as simply Scottish literature. The overseas writers with whom Morgan deals are passionately involved with their countries' cultural and political lives. Zbigniew Herbert and Mayakovsky are poets whose own work is politically engaged yet aesthetically rigorous, part of the changing nature of their cultures. Something of the same could be said of Morgan's output.

There is no one cultural entity called Scotland that lasts through the ages. Scotland is an amalgam, a constructed assembly of cultures and languages; it is reinvented from age to age; it is an 'imagined community'. Where 18th-century Scots strove to create a British (as distinct from English) literature, 20th-century Scottish writers aim, on the whole, for a post-British identity that is particularly Scottish in a new way. MacDiarmid's way was Anglophobic, a strident rewriting of the story of Scotland as encyclopedic and fierce, internationally-oriented and chauvinistically macho. MacDiarmid's Scotland now appears curiously antique, its anachronistic nature highlighted in his eulogy of authentically 'Scottish' pubs which are "men only", as opposed to "meretricious deScotticised" bars where "Men (if you can call them that) even take their wives and daughters along with them". Perhaps necessary in its time, MacDiarmid's view of Scottish culture and literature is now seriously out of date, an object of study and passionate stimulus, but not a *credo* for any but the most conservative of contemporary Scots. Part of the subtle courage of Morgan's criticism comes from an implicit realisation that this is so.

Though he has written some of the best criticism of MacDiarmid's later poetry, and though deeply sympathetic towards the 'MacDiarmid Embattled' of whom he wrote in 1959, Morgan responded warmly in 1972 to a climate in which "old polarities do not command the devotion they did". Writing of the Citizens' Theatre in his *TLS* survey of 'The Resources of Scotland', he uses the adjectives "alien and unScottish" almost as terms of praise. In this piece and many of the essays in his 1990 volume, *Crossing the Border*, there is a sense that he sees the need for a more generous, less embattled approach to Scotland's histories and literatures. He is able to build on MacDiarmid's legacy without being incarcerated in it. If Morgan writes as a nationalist critic, he does not allow his politics to blind him, and he sees the ultimate grounding of nationalist convictions not in terms of a kind of military offensive, but simply in terms of self-respect: "There comes a time when out of respect for itself a country must collect its resources, and look at its assets and shortcomings with an eye that is both sharp and warm: see what is there, what is not there, what could be there." Scotland's artists have often helped in this exemplary task. MacDiarmid performed the operation with fire and brimstone, but Morgan is able to conduct it with an eminently reasonable smile. While MacDiarmid's audience was frequently antagonised, this could scarcely be said of Morgan's readers. One of the achievements of Morgan's criticism is it clears the way for the debating and examination of both Scottishness and Scottish literature in a non-gladiatorial atmosphere, without abandoning a nationalist impetus.

Morgan has achieved this not least through his work as an academic at Glasgow University. His job allowed him to spend time considering his country's heritage and in a climate less polemical and sketchy than that of journalism. It also encouraged him to develop his intellectual equipment, rather than just pumping up the Dylan Thomas rhetoric present in some of his earliest poetic efforts. Morgan's academic career surely shaped all his writing. So many of his poems are puzzles, or reflections on the course of history. Despite his statements in interviews, he cares greatly for the past. The poet of *Sonnets from Scotland* is very much concerned with nodes of energy in the traditions of Scottish culture, as is Morgan the critic. 'Wittgenstein on Egdon Heath' and the sonnet opening, "Yes, I taught Milton. He was a sharp boy", suggest a poet who likes to play in an openly bookish environment, and who (like MacDiarmid) has the courage of his intellect and his reading. However, where the later MacDiarmid often used his learning to intimidate, the more openly ludic Morgan converts his hours in the library into poetry that is accessibly entertaining.

His job, largely, enriched his verse; otherwise, as he has said, he would have given it up. Undoubtedly, at times, it also had deleterious effects on his creativity. He rejoices in his 'Hantle of Howlers', but also falls victim to the stifling force of producing (and suggesting answers to) exam questions: "*The Anatomist* (1930) and *The Slab Boys* (1978) are obviously two very different plays, but they do have certain things in common, and they make an interesting comparison." This opening sentence of his 1987 piece 'James Bridie's *The Anatomist* and John Byrne's *The Slab Boys*' reads like the start of something competent and dull. Morgan was aware of the complexities of being both poet and academic, as he explained in a 1959 symposium in *Universities Quarterly* (reprinted in *Nothing Not Giving Messages*):

> The university writer discovers that he must guard a certain modicum of unassimilability; even if he is a good teacher, he must not allow himself merely to 'become' a university teacher - he has to keep, and fiercely keep, the kind of independence that every writer has by nature. In so far as a university is an absorbing and protecting world of its own, he must gently fight it.

Morgan is striving to achieve the position of an insider-outsider, a stance sought by numerous 20th-century writers. Though he was a fine teacher and a conscientious tutor, there were aspects of Morgan's creative life he felt obliged to shield from academia. His job intensified his position as an insider-outsider. Though now a Visiting Professor teaching Scottish Literature at the University of Strathclyde, he taught at Glasgow as a member of the Department of English, not Scottish, literature. He taught virtually no Scottish texts. Many of his essays on Scottish Literature in *Crossing the Border* were first given not at Glasgow, but as visiting lectures, or papers delivered to the Association for Scottish Literary Studies. His teaching position must have enriched his reading - Milton, Emily Bronte, Poe and Hopkins are among many welcome visitors received by his poetry as well as his prose, but his energies may have been further split by the fact that his teaching duties concentrated on non-Scottish literature.

Perhaps a certain fissuring of his academic activities explains Morgan's odd lack of interest in the theories of structuralism and poststructuralism which were being so forcefully developed elsewhere during his time at Glasgow. Though an enthusiast for French and Russian poetry, as well as one of the few Scottish poets who has read with obvious interest the work of Ashbery and of the L=A=N=G=U=A=G=E poets, Morgan in his criticism ignores alike Barthes and Derrida, Bakhtin and Todorov. In the volume of critical essays *About Edwin Morgan*, Jack Rillie points out that when Morgan became a professional academic the prevailing ethos remained essentially Arnoldian. In his 'computer poems' and in his sequence of 'Unfinished Poems' written in memory of Veronica Forest-Thomson, he shows some interest in structuralism, but the lack of such concerns in his criticism is particularly surprising in the work of a fluent reader of Russian and French and a active university teacher. Where one might have expected to see applications of new critical methodologies to Scottish literature, there is a strange blank. His critical writings, while strengthened by insights born of his own poetic practice, are conservative in style, ignoring the -isms, whether of feminism or poststructuralism. For many in Scotland and beyond, this is reassuring. His often exemplary influence on younger Scottish critics may, however, have resulted in the isolation of Scottish criticism from internationally-recognised developments in critical theory. Certainly there seems a generally low level of theoretical awareness among the 'ScotLit' community (Alan Riach may be something of an exception).

Morgan's very eschewing of critical theory may, nevertheless, have been linked purposefully to an awareness that the immediate, and even medium-term requirements of Scottish literary scholarship were most of all for a fully-enunciated literary history. His 1971 essay 'Towards a Literary History' (which, significantly, opens *Crossing the Border*) demonstrates his view that "The case for a history of Scottish literature may have to be made with an air of being out of phase with critical developments against such histories". As Scots "we have a duty to ourselves to do what the Americans have done: to map out, as part of their own nationhood, what their literary history means to them". His essay can be seen as a forerunner of the histories of Scottish .literature produced since, like the one-volume *Literature of Scotland* by Roderick Watson and the sometimes uneven four-volume *History of Scottish Literature* published under the general editorship of Cairns Craig. It is probable that in the long term Morgan's backing of the need for a new history of Scottish literature will be seen as a valid position, particularly given the awkwardness of combining a nationalist stance with a deconstructionist one. Nevertheless, it would be good to see more Scottish critics who were prepared to debate that awkwardness, and more creative writers whose knowledge and intellectual equipment were sufficient to engage with such questions in their reinvention of a postmodern Scotland.

The danger of Morgan's critical stance is that it leaves a legacy of critical conservatism which may in the long run inhibit the development of Scottish creative writing, or at least the full appreciation of it in Scotland and beyond. We must not have a Scottish critical kailyard.

Morgan backed the idea of a new literary history of Scotland, but he did not provide such a history. His own essays cover scattered, if related, topics. Some of the best of them (such as the pieces on 'Dunbar and the Language of Poetry' and on 'Voice, Tone and Transition in *Don Juan*') relate to themes which have a bearing on his own poetry. He celebrates the mercurial and constantly changing qualities of these writers, at the same time as seeing in them a fundamental integrity. He uses the adjective 'elusive' with relish. He is attracted to the urban sensibility of Fergusson, Garioch, and contemporary Glaswegian writers. He admires the experimentalism of Dunbar and even Drummond, as well as that of Carlyle, MacDiarmid, Graham, Findlay, and Tom Leonard. Yet, particularly in the writings of an advocate of the need for a Scottish literary history, there are some very odd omissions. The most obvious among these is Robert Burns.

Though there are about a dozen references to Burns scattered through *Crossing the Border*, Morgan avoids those greatest of iconic producers of Scottishness, the authors of 'Tam o'Shanter' and *Waverley*. These evasions are unfortunate, but deliberate. Morgan has been asked if he wished to write a history of Scottish literature, but he has declined. *Crossing the Border* is subtitled *Essays on Scottish Literature*; it would be wrong to expect a continuous history. The first essay gestures in the direction of literary history, and other pieces deal with a wide variety of male Scottish authors from Dunbar to Leonard. The omission of Burns and Scott, not to mention Henryson and Hogg, is surprising and, in many ways disappointing. One would welcome from Morgan an essay on Hogg.

He writes well on Scottish authors, argues from a quietly nationalist perspective, yet does not come coherently to grips with the ways in which Scottishness has been articulated. A more fully-developed deployment of literary theory would help this, indeed would demand it. It may seem grudging to examine Morgan's criticism in this way, but his essays are so full of tempting suggestions that one wishes they were followed further. "To Joyce, Carlyle was one of the great liberators of language", Morgan contends in 'Carlyle's Style", and such a view of Carlyle as a proto-Modernist is surely worthwhile. But he does not really make out a case. He sees that the need for a Scottish literary history is the need for a *revisionary* history which will contribute both to Scottish self-respect and to a potent rearrangement of literatures in English. His essays contain, like MacDiarmid's, stray hints of this. The fragments, however, are never assembled.

Morgan's essays are just that - tries, attempts, often highly acute ones, rather than sustained and developed views of his culture and its literature. His criticism, like T S Eliot's, often appears a by-product of his own poetry workshop. To say this is not to slight the criticism but to place it in exalted company, for as poet-critic eminent in his own culture Morgan is author of an impressive dual achievement. The critical essays are useful and important in the interpreting and siting of Morgan's own verse, as are the anthologies which he has edited. Yet to see them as only that is to undervalue them. For, whatever its shortcomings, Morgan's position as a critic has been importantly instrumental in effecting within the discussion of Scottish writing a transition from the isolated polemic of MacDiarmid to the more reasonable debate carried out in a growing critical community that includes writers and academics as well as those who are neither. To be thankful for this transition is not to eschew all polemics (Scotland would be the poorer without its various forms of flyting, as Morgan points out), but it is to celebrate a climate in which sustained growth is more probable.

Maybe Morgan has managed to combine a nationalist stance with something of the splendid catholicity of taste which could be displayed by the critic Edwin Muir. If MacDiarmid was an embattled individual trying often to present himself as part of some larger movement, Morgan can more easily and undemonstratively ground himself as part of a Scottish cultural community. He uses the pronoun 'we', meaning 'we Scots', with unforced ease, a sign perhaps of the cultural self-respect which his own work strengthens. His continuing presence at the heart of so many Scottish literary debates has been a positive factor in the development of the literary institutions of a country many of whose writers live beyond its bounds. A constant speaker at conferences and other gatherings to do with Scottish literature, Morgan has occupied a critical position which has enhanced cultural self-respect and confidence while keeping an eye on foreign poetic developments and stressing the need for an international perspective. So his work may be set alongside not only other contributions to modern Scottish literary criticism, but also such developments in Scottish art criticism as the magazine *Alba* and the writings of Duncan MacMillan.

It is difficult to live as a critic in Scotland, even as a poet-critic. Morgan was fortunate in being able to combine an academic career with his other writing activities. He has been fortunate also in his publishers. Contemporary Scottish critics have a reasonable range of publishing opportunities open to them, particularly if their work is suited to an academic market. I hope that the climate which Morgan's criticism has helped to create and the brighter publishing prospects prevailing in Scottish letters will see not only a growth in the quantity but also an increase in the sophistication of Scottish criticism. But important Scottish work is still not available in book-form. It is to be regretted, for instance, that Douglas Dunn has not so far published a volume of his critical essays. While Dunn is generally of a more conservative literary temperament than Morgan, and is notably hostile to the recent upsurge of interest in literary theory, his range of concerns in Scottish writing and beyond, combined with his experience of the international literary arena, could enhance the attention given to Scottish criticism as well as creative writing. If work such as Dunn's criticism can be collected in book form, and if other, more theoretically-aware Scottish critics - including, please, feminist critics and literary historians - can develop, contest and build upon the insights of Morgan's essays, then his work as a poet-critic will stand not just for itself, but also as a crucial bridge from the prose of MacDiarmid to a pluralistic Scottish criticism of the future.

Robert Crawford

*Edwin Morgan, coloured pencil on cream paper
by Alexander Moffat, Photograph by Tom Scott*

Translations by Edwin Morgan

from the Hungarian of Atilla József (1905-37)

ANT

The ant asleep among the chrysalises:
may the wind blow lightly through the chrysalises now!
Or not, it would still be all right.

Its small exhausted head is propped on a glitter of mica
and its tiny shadow lies asleep by its side.

Take a straw to wake him gently!
But really we should start off home,
heavy clouds hang -

An ant asleep among the chrysalises
and - plop! - the first drop already on my hand.

SITTING, STANDING, KILLING, DYING

Pushing this chair away from me,
crouching where a train will be,
climbing a mountain with great care,
shaking my sack down clefts of air,
giving my ancient spider honey,
keeping an aged woman sunny,
supping on bean-soup, hot and good,
tiptoeing through yards of mud,
laying my hat on the railway-line,
circling the lake in my own time,
sitting clothed at the bottom of it,
blushing through waves that ring and glint,
blossoming among the sunflowers -
or simply sighing easy hours,
simply brushing off a fly,
dusting my book to put it by -
spitting dead centre in my mirror,
converting enemies with peaceful fervour,
killing them all with a long blade,
watching how pools of blood are made,
seeing how little girls turn round -
or simply sitting here, as if bound -
setting all Budapest alight,
waiting with crumbs for birds to alight,
throwing my wretched bread on the ground,
making my dear lover shout and pound,
popping her little sister on my lap,
and if I must pay the world for that,
leaving a bill that's as blind as a bat -

O you, making me tie and untie,
now making me write this poetry,
you, still making me laugh and cry,
my life, making me pick and try!

POSTCARD FROM PARIS

The *patron* always lets me sleep in,
Bertha becomes Jeanette in Paris,
and there's hot spinach for everyone,
lighted candles on sale at the barber's.

Saint Michel sports sixty naked
women singing to the sky,
and Notre Dame: you shiver and shake there,
or spend five francs to see me from on high.

At night the Eiffel Tower collapses
and snuggles into misty sheets,
and the *gendarmes* kiss the lasses
and the toilets have no seats.

SINGING TO ONESELF

Road and meadow swim at peace
through the heart of chilly seas
horo
through the heart of chilly seas -
Potatoes and spoon to get us by,
in filth we live, in filth we die
horo
in filth we live, in filth we die -
Down in the mouth, my little son?
I'll think a new shirt on you soon
horo
I'll think a new shirt on you soon -
No one is his, he has no one to grieve for,
whom the Party alone is on the *qui vive* for
horo
whom the Party alone is on the *qui vive* for -

ÁRON JÓZSEF MY FATHER

Áron József my father,
soap-boiler, now he
wafts scent, scyther
of grass on the Great Sea.
Borcse Pöcze my mother,
cancer ate her, hundred-

legged scrubbing-brushes
struck at belly and stomach.

And Luca, I loved her,
but she never loved me.
My furniture - a shadow.
My friends - none to see.

My fears and feuds are over,
melted into my soul -
I live now for ever
a dull self, alone.

EPITAPH FOR A SPANISH FARM-HAND

General Franco made me one of his crack troops,
  fear of the firing-squad ensured I was no deserter.
It was fear that kept me fighting justice and freedom
  at the walls of Irun. Death found me all the same.

from the Chinese of Li Po (702-762)

MURNIN O THE MERCHES-GAIRD

By the Nor'Yett, the wund blaws fu o saun,
Lanelie fae time's jizzen tae thir days!
The wid crines, the gress yallas at hairst.
I sclim tours an tours
    tae vizzy the barbour straths:
Oorie barmekin, the lift, the braid desart.
Nae waw stauns noo i this clachan.
Banes blanchit wi a thoosan forsts,
Hie-humphit deid-knoks, owrheildit wi trees an gress;
Wha brung uz thir effeirs?
Wha brung the levin o the cankert coorts?
Wha brung the airmy wi its touk an tarantara?
Barbour keengs.
A douce spring, cheengit tae bluid-gowpin hairst.
A stramash o fechters, spreed owr this haill kintra,
Three hunner an saxty thoosan,
An dool, dool lik dash an dag.
Dool awaw, an dool, dool at retour.
Toom, toom faulds,
Wi nae a chiel o the fecht upo them,
    Nae langer birkies tae gaird or tae breenge.
Och, hoo sall ye ken the doolie wae at the Nor'Yett,
Wi oor ledar Li Mu's name negleckit,
An uz, the gairdsmen, fother for teegers.

(from Ezra Pound's 'Lament of the Frontier Guard' (1914), itself a
translation from the Chinese of Li Po.)

Morganmania

Angus Calder

Heinrich Heine coined the term 'Lisztomania' to convey the excitement surrounding the virtuoso composer-pianist's tours in the 1840s, from Turkey to Ireland, Russia to Portugal: in 1840-1, Liszt played 45 concerts in 31 towns within 67 days, and travelled over 2,000 miles to do this, everywhere acclaimed with something not unlike 'Beatlemania'. The result? Hard to summarise, but, very probably, a distinct shift in European sensibility.

Edwin Morgan perhaps speaks better Hungarian than Liszt, who learnt the language of his native land only late in life, but whose name may well have inspired Morgan's 'Siesta of a Hungarian Snake.' The translator of Sándor Weöres (and Heine) has also travelled to Turkey to perform, and the experiments of Portuguese-speaking Brazilian Concrete Poets inspired his own 'concrete' ventures (including 'Siesta'). He has an intensely Romantic sensibility, and is, of course, a virtuoso performer. In 1990 the European Capital of Culture was gripped by Morganmania. The poet's seventieth birthday happily coincided with Glasgow's ceremonial marriage to the Muses. Newspaper articles and public occasions fumbled to assert Morgan's centrality (somehow) to Glasgow Culture. The result? Well, a distinct shift in Scottish sensibility was, surely, being registered?

Morgan as Culture Hero of Noemeancity? A University Professor? A come-out gay? A man interested in many, many things, but not apparently in football? A friendly man, but systematically non-gregarious, neither a joiner of Parties nor a reveller at parties? And a constant, even aggressive opponent of the nostalgia for vanished tenements and rust-belt technology which suffused much of Glasgow 1990, as it has done so much recent writing about the city? Most improbable. But what good news - a flying fish, a swimming bird, a branched and breering contradiction, great fun: Edwin the Angle, King of Northumbria, spliced with Morgan, Welsh from British Strathclyde, to produce a wholly native graft bearing strange fruits. A makar alert to the whole of the long tradition of craftsmanship in Scots, who nevertheless writes primarily in English, or in languages of his own invention, whose favourite novel (it seems) is *Wuthering Heights* and who'd rather have Milton than Burns with him on a desert island.

No poet is so much 'taught' in Scottish schools, or so well known in person in those grim places: though less spectacular, his travels to them under the SAC scheme must, year in year out, have equalled *in toto* Liszt's mileages noted above. Yet his most popular poems with young people are about a vicious gangster ('King Billy') and a blind hunchback peeing 'In the Snack Bar'. There is no poet more learned in ancient Latin and sixties aesthetics, more 'academic' in his erudition: but who communicates better in public reading, who grabs the resistant tyro faster? And who has more contempt (albeit gently expressed) for those who would explain such paradoxes with big talk of Calvinist hangovers, 'English imperialism', crises in Scottish consciousness, antisyzygies . . . Come to think of it, that Hungarian snake is an antisyzygy, surely? Harmless, serenely at rest, a creature tamed by Orpheus: s sz sz SZ sz SZ sz ZS zs ZS zs zs z

In 1990, for just under £85 (rather more than a boxed set of Wagner's *Ring* on cassette, but below the price of a flight to Amsterdam, a city not without special meaning for Morgan) one could purchase a Morgankit in four volumes, though not quite so complete as it looked at first sight.

The *Collected Poems*, which don't require 'review' here, omit quite a lot of work from earlier volumes, as well as those erotica which Morgan tantalisingly avers won't be published in his lifetime. (And one still has to seek his translations in many scattered places.) The limply titled *Crossing the Border* (presumably, it evokes the Auden-Britten choo-choo in the Grierson-Watt film *Night Mail*: but Morgan has lived in Scotland all his life, except for army service) collects the criticism of Scottish writers from Dunbar to Tom Leonard, but for his critical thoughts on non-caledonian makars, dramatists and novelists one will have to turn to the volume of *Essays* which Carcanet published in 1974, or go to the NLS for, eg, Morgan's 1979 Warton Lecture on '"Sublime and Alarming" Images in Poetry'. I haven't had time to do this yet, but learn of it through the bibliography of works by and about Morgan constructed by Hamish Whyte for Edinburgh University Press's festschrift, where it takes up 115 pages, and nearly half the volume - despite which, Whyte has to admit that it's not comprehensive.

About Edwin Morgan is the best edited of the three prose volumes: a book of very practical use not only to future critics but also to mere readers of poetry anxious to understand Morgan better (though EM himself, quoting Coleridge, would warn the latter that "when no criticism is pretended to . . . the poetry gives most pleasure when only generally and not perfectly understood.") Besides searching scholarly contributions, there is an acute biographical introduction by Kevin McCarra, essays of special interest by Iain Crichton Smith and Douglas Dunn, a sensible piece about 'teaching' Morgan in schools by Geddes Thomson, and a modest and vivid account by Robin Hamilton of being Morgan's student at Glasgow University in the sixties: the prime of Mr EM, but even in this happy period the master did not drop his guard, his self-effacing reticence about his own life and work.

That guard is dropped, with a very loud noise, in *Nothing Not Giving Messages*, an odd but fascinating book which begins with an inventory of objects, books, records in Morgan's flat in Anniesland, taken by the editor Hamish Whyte on 4 July 1989 (was the transatlantic resonance fortuitous?) and ends with a list kept by 'EM' himself of books read between 1927 and May 1940, an odyssey from G A Henty and Percy Westerman to T S Eliot, V Woolf and the great 19th century Russians. Part I reprints nine interviews conducted in the 70s and 80s by various persons and Part II collects articles, statements, lectures, in which the poet talks about his craft and his life: "The Don as Poet . . . the Poet's Working Day . . . What it Feels Like to be a Scottish Poet . . . Poets in Schools . . . Poet in Person . . ." etc etc.

The 1988 interview by Christopher Whyte suddenly transforms everything - lighting up with an almost lurid flash the cagey responses to questions printed before it, in this volume, and illuminating the wary attitude towards 'Scottish tradition' found in the essays in *Crossing the Border*. It's not just that Morgan talks about being gay explicitly for the first time in 'prose' (one could have deduced that from certain poems long since). It's the gusto with which he recalls his gay life, along with the candour with which he recognises that his attitudes, including his inhibitions, belong to his own generation, born unluckily long pre-Wolfenden, but, luckily, matured before AIDS. References elsewhere to writers' block in the forties, unhappiness in the fifties, can now be specifically related to his sexuality - but Morgan allows for historical contingencies as well, refuses to let his own gayness dominate his perspective of society and history.

It's not just being gay that counts, it's where you're gay (Glasgow, Scotland, middle-class) and what's happening around you. The 30s, Morgan remarks in his essay 'MacDiarmid's Later Poetry' (1978), were not truly a "political and socio-economic decade . . . In terms of the life of mind . . . it was a decade when other things were more central: in particular, biology and time, the link between these being probably the idea of evolution, though there was also much interest in dreams and precognition. There was a new attempt to see man in the round, in a cosmic rather than social setting . . ." Behind Morgan we must clearly hear not just Mayakovsky, Pound, Ginsberg, Carlos Williams and so on but the fiction of Wells and Verne and the popular 'science-writing' of the decade in which that category of journalism was invented. However, it is important to know that Morgan learnt much about art and life from a gay student whom his parents, with endearing incaution, employed to teach him piano and Latin in his teens. Lex Allan was full of news about gay poets - Auden, Spender, Lorca. He was also, like these poets, 'political'. And it was Morgan's infatuation with a young, alas heterosexual, Communist which led him to Russian classes at Glasgow University . . .

Just so, there is no doubt that Morgan's belated surge of mature creativity which brought him international recognition in the 1960s was energised by his first wholly successful romance, with a Catholic storeman, John Scott. But which came first - the widespread feeling from the outset of that decade that everything new was possible, and everything possible new, the verse of the Beats, the music of the Beatles? Or was it that his 'second life' prime of sexual fulfilment - 'joy' - a word he uses with telling effect - enabled him to sort himself out in relation to the new, cultural influences, to seize a moment of history which was *his* as much as JFK's, Ian Hamilton Findlay's, Richard Demarco's, John Cage's, Holub's, Vosznesensky's?

Such questions intrigue Morgan himself. He tells Whyte: "If you're of my generation your power is in some way linked with the fact that there are these undeclared feelings and, if they were fully declared, you might lose some of your power." Even in the sixties, Morgan couldn't 'come out'. But what 'came out' of Morgan was new power, charging experiments based on radically different, even incompatible formal aesthetics. 'In the Snack Bar', as 'social realism', stands about half way between the impersonality of Concrete Poetry and the quivering Romantic sensualism of 'Strawberries'. He also produced collage poems; 'instamatic' poems attempting to 'document' bizarre episodes found in newspapers (very much in the spirit of Surrealism, another '30s' influence on the poet); 'sound poems', 'computer

poems'; sonnets; 'science fiction' space poems; and I wot not what - a whole
department-store with toys for kiddies, leisure wear for young lovers and
useful wares for responsible adults. ('Approved by the Matthew Arnold Good
Housekeeping Institute' or 'Made in Europe: Guaranteed Socially Relevant'.)

Enough of this flippancy. Morgan is one of our major writers. "In spite of
all temptations to belong to other nations," he remains Glaswegian - and, as
Robin Hamilton's memoir shows, was quietly central to the emergence in the
60s of Glasgow's first-ever identifiable 'school' of writers. He regrets the
exile of W S Graham, the first poet he knew personally - "someone who
came from Greenock and Glasgow ought not to have lived so long in a
telephoneless cottage in the wilds of Cornwall." And for all Morgan's
healthy insistence that present and future are what matter - past and
tradition be damned - his critical essays make it easy for us to relate him to
earlier Scottish writers.

In an important early essay on Dunbar, (1952) he writes of that Makar's
"agility . . . virtuosity in tempo and momentum . . . glancing and headlong
jugglery" - the author of 'Cinquevalli' connives in the old poet's delight in
"words with no matter" at the expense of serious Chaucerian moralising. He
writes with gusto about Robert Garioch's meeting with Houdini - his
Edinburgh friend too was a great 'escapologist'. "The quickness with which
Byron sees the potential of a new word" is one aspect of *Don Juan* which
Morgan praises in a wonderfully observant essay: he revels also in Carlyle's
"barbarous" neologisms and the "heady pleasures of excess" generated by
MacDiarmid's "enormous risks with vocabulary". And he can quote a poem
by William Fowler, one of James VI's Castalian Band, which already, in the
late 16th century, looks like something only Morgan could have written:

> my sight aux vents, mes pleurs unto the seas.
> my flames to feu, mes gazings unto your ees.

Repressed sexual energy's common enough: addiction to languages and
dictionaries isn't. But here's another paradox. *Nothing Not Giving Messages*
looks like the title of a Barthesian tract in post-structuralist semiotics, by
one of those tricksy theoretical critics who aver that authors are written by
texts and that the vaunted subjectivities of the former are merely
ideological constructions. Of this kind of 'criticism' Morgan will have none.
Even the sculpture-poems of Finlay, striving for semiotic absoluteness, he
relates to the artist's personality. Revelling in the surfaces and interfaces of
discourses, registers, genres, structures, Morgan still challenges us to find
Morgan himself, his true biography, in his multifarious poetic output.

Well, what of the man? Everything in these volumes confirms one's
impression of him in person, at readings, in those brief but pointful convers-
ations which this friendly but most reserved of men indulges us with before
whizzing off as fast as he decently can back to base, back to the dictionaries,
the omnivorous reading, the restless writing, the Beatles records, the
newspaper cuttings, the videos of *Star Wars*, at home in Anniesland. Morgan
is balanced, humane, almost incapable of uttering a cliche, yet never one to
flaunt intellectualism. He is always clear: clear even about the 'mystery' he
insists is there at the core of aesthetic experience, of poetic inspiration and
achievement. He has no time for Gods or dogmas, credits no afterlife,

delights in the immediate, the material and the mundane, and preserves intact the Wellsian faith of his youth, that science and technology are good things in themselves and in no way alien to poetry. Above all, he values *energy*: that quality manifested when mild Professor Morgan suddenly launches out on the platform as Loch Ness Monster or Mummy or Mercurian, juggles with words like Cinquevalli, plucks his lexical guitar with Little Blue Blue, invades Heaven with Jack London or grumbles in a Glasgow video box near the close where the shilpit dog fucks grimly. Even that dog, *such* energy . . . like the trio in 'Trio', like the hard man on 'Glasgow Green'.

In his conversation with Whyte, dizzying speculation is joyfully unleashed. "Glasgow's said to be the bisexual centre of the universe", remarks Morgan - and goes on to exemplify this from his own experience: for instance, that the Glasgow hard man can be very gay indeed after his fashion. He agrees with Whyte that a theme linking the 'Glasgow school', found in Leonard's and Lochhead's work, is an "interest in what it means to be male or female."

Perhaps the instant appeal of Morgan's varied verse has most to do with the uncensorious, compassionate curiosity with which he projects human vitalities, joyful, vicious, ambiguous, male, female ('Goddesses' is one of his best sequences.) Perhaps that is 'it'. Is 'it' especially Scottish . . . ? If so, we are other than we have thought. History and tradition must be reconstructed. One might start by reconsidering that remarkable love, borne by the Douglas towards the Bruce, which led the former to heroics and death in Spain. We might also ask why our local monster is 'Nessie' and why, alone in western Europe, our men wear skirts . . .

I was about to write "to conclude with a serious point" . . . But I think my last point is not un-serious. 'Morganmania' does bring with it a re-examination of ourselves - a forward-looking optimism, a merry view of Scotland, and shared laughter. We can't all be gay but we can all try to be gayer. Morgan, as Geddes Thomson writes, "is, first of all, a poet of the present, of the headline in today's newspaper, of things that are happening here and now." And, here and now, he is a wonderful antidote to over-solemn broodings - about, for instance, our "relations with England" and "relations with Europe", both of which, as Morgan exemplifies, can be great fun. The more languages, dialects and idiolects we can use, the less Standard English will bother us. Behind all, as Morgan reminds us, quoting Walter Benjamin, is the "true language" in which all poetry is written, existing independently of all particular tongues, awaiting release by original writer and then by translator alike . . . "At times," Morgan writes, "when states are anxious to establish their national identity and to prove the virtues of their language, they have very often in history indulged in widespread translation from other cultures; yet in the process of doing this they subtly alter their own language, joining it in many unforeseen ways to a greater continent of almost undefined and non-specific human expression."

Angus Calder

Edwin Morgan, *Collected Poems*, Carcanet, £25; *Crossing the Border: Essays on Scottish Literature*, Carcanet, £25; *Nothing Not Giving Messages: Reflections on his work and life*, Polygon, £14.95; Robert Crawford & Hamish Whyte (eds), *About Edwin Morgan*, Edinburgh University Press, £19.50

Stuart McHardy

Solstice.
Breathe
each breath a circle
like the circle of time
in this the dark time
sleep of seeding
breath grows shorter
in the pulsing of this time
this day the circle stops
at the darkest hour
the circle stops
breathless
as the world again begins.

INITIATION

Deep i the nicht
i the toom mirk oor,
i the toom mirk oor
o the nicht's deep dairk
comes a soond
like watter on stane
comes a soond
like steel on bane
an oorie sound o eldritch pain,
Come oot, come oot ye cannae hide
as an oolet hoots frae the ither side
come oot, come oot an face yer weird
wi sichtless een an bane-filled beard
come oot, come oot the time has come
there is nae place that ye can run;
ye cleik a stane, it turns tae sand
ungraspable bi ony hand,
an aa the watters o time await
tae see gif ye maun dree yer fate;
yer nerves're on fire, yer bluid's i spate
like ye'd been ca'd tae yer ain wake,
the sheddaes that eddy an twist aroon
that come straucht frae the mooth o doom
cannae hide yer sicht or smell
frae the red-lugged dugs wha mate i hell
they're here at yer bid like aa the rest
slaverin, tae waatch ye tak the test;
so here ye stand, alane, unaidit,
yer body washed, yer hair new-braidit

an gif ye can fir three lang days
remain a man
thro terror an horror an unbid sichts
mang grugous gangrel mochie lichts
an gif ye can lowse aa yer fears
fecht them doon an beat them clear
bi standin, wi nae thocht o flicht
at last ye'll come tae mornin's licht
an the sang o a quine by watterside
yer hairt clean free an yer hands untied.

THE PROFESSIONS

It's said the first profession was that o the hoor
an aa likelihood points tae her bein poor
bit gettin siller in her haund gied the men a fricht
so they inventit a polisman tae lock thir fear up ticht,
an then anither, cleverer man, thinkin o the gowd
made up bein a lawyer, an he felt michty proud
then the polis an the lawyer they thocht a little while
an aa the time the poor lass was stuck inside the jile,
an jobs bein jobs, an greed bein greed
the jile filled up wi ither quines wha'd likewise been in need:
Then the lawyer and the polis saw this couldna jist keep on
so they found a daft auld dottled man an Lo the judge was born:
So the quines were tried, an they were fined, then in the streets again
they'd ply their trade a little while, an ye ken whit happened then,
the polis they'd arrest them the lawyer'd take a fee
the auld judge he wad tak his share an set the lassies free,
the circle it went on an on, richt up till the day
a woman finds a means o work, but it's men wha mak it pay.

THE BACK O THE HAA

The cry came up, unlooked for
frae near the back o the haa
the place whaur the puir fowk hunker
wha bide 'tween the win an the waa,
'Whit is this *we* ye haver
as yer wards grease the bools i yer mooth?
ye've nivver felt hungrin's slaver
yer 'we' kens naethin o drooth,
thon terrible drooth fir freedom
tae hae things the 'wey *we* wad like
wi'oot yer political con games
that only suroon us wi' dykes

there, tae mak siccar that leadin
bides jist as it is, fir the few
an the mony ahent ye proceedin
jist bigg up their prison anew:
But as ye gie yer aa fir the nation
yer jist like the rest o yer ilk
payin fir yer bairns' education
an dressin yer douce wife i silk,
an then ye come back an ye tell us
we're aa o us on the ae side
bit we ken whit ye're tryin tae sell us
an we ken how aften ye've tried,
an ivver ye mind us o freedom
but yer freedom's no worth a toss
for we hae oor ain sort o wisdom
an ken politics is no just a cross
scrieved on a wee bittie paper
every five years or so,
that yer club can continue tae function
an yer influence continue tae grow.
Still ye cam back an tell us we're British
an remind us o aa ye hae done
but as soon as the coontin is finished
we ken fine whaur it is ye will run:
back tae the Bigtoon like lightnin
tae strut an tae pose mang yer freens
siccar ye've maistered the recknin
o pooer, o wealth an o dreams.
An back here we're aince mair forlieten
like a backyaird fair throttlit wi weeds
oor problems no warth o meetin
an mickle concern fir oor needs,
then ye fill up oor land wi corruption
wasteland, pollution an guns
an oor cities again ken starvation
an aince mair the rickets returns.
We ken weel that this is yer midden
whaur aa things unsichtly are hid
but thistles aye grow best unbidden
like the white hind that's deep i the wid,
so ye can tak yer fine wards an orations
an keep playin at yer auld game
ilk day there's mair see yer fictions
created i guid freedom's name,
an we ken fine whit it is ye are daein
claimin tae wark fir us aa
can ye no hear the chainlinks snappin
up here at the back o the haa?   Stuart McHardy

Christine McNeill

The Lesson

A tap on the letter slot.

He hangs his leather jacket up in the hall. She makes a gesture towards the front room. He follows, sits down on the sofa.

She insisted on the direct method. Introducing the vocabulary, repeating each word three times, pausing, if necessary standing up and performing a mime.

Purpose of wanting to learn German? To take up an army post in Heidelberg.

She smiled, and said: "Der Vater. The V pronounced like an F."

She listened to his creative endeavours: "Der Vater geht . . ." - The father goes . . . "Der Vater wohnt . . ." - The father lives . . .

"Sehr gut," she complimented him. Then nodded at his pages of script. "Der Vater ist tot." She leant back. Enjoying his struggle in trying to grasp the last word.

"Tot." She let her head go slack. Then drew a large black cross on a piece of paper.

Her own father, Herr Johann Genz, had been an ordinary bank clerk, belonging to an ordinary political group in Vienna. She was a child, when one day the neighbours told her: "Your father has been hanged!"

At night she imagined it. That rope attached to the bedroom curtain. Moving towards the shadow cast by the chair near her bed. The weave was thick and methodical. Above her bed it went limp, then looped itself. "Der Vater ist tot." In the morning, the rope hung again at the side of the curtain.

"Ah." Eagerly he consigned the word "tot" to his memory.

She watched him. Remembering 1947. Next door lived a friend by the name of Karl. She, Miri, in those days, used to give him half her bread.

One day, after the defeat of the Austrian and German army, a Russian had come to her mother's flat. He had returned the following day with a giant loaf. Her mother and she had shared it, and offered some to Karl's mother. But Karl's mother had rejected it, and also told Karl not to take any. Why, she'd asked. Karl had looked at the ground. Then he had said: "There is a rumour that your mother didn't get the bread just for allowing the Russian to wash his hands."

"He was so grateful," she'd said.

Karl had looked at her with fierce eyes. "Miri, he was a Russian! One can't let an enemy into one's home. All the other tenants were mad about it."

"They didn't say anything."

"They were mad at your mother."

"Mother didn't tell me."

"Then I will tell you: my mother said your mother didn't get the bread just for the water."

"What do you mean?"

"My mother said your mother took her clothes off."

"Took her clothes off? I don't understand."

"She was naked!"

"Why?"

"Ask your mother."

The student looked at her, expectant for the next word.

"Mutter," she said. "The u pronounced like the English double o."

She rather liked him. She asked him to stand up. She wanted him to look in the mirror and describe his appearance.

Gossip. People talked, telling a story over and over, and by the time it had traversed three or four months, a Rabelaisian story came out.

"You didn't take your clothes off for him?"

"Of course not," her mother said.

"Then why do people say it?"

"They say it because they do not trust us."

"That's no reason to tell lies."

Her mother had brushed breadcrumbs from the table. "People tell lies, when they're afraid of their own truth."

"Verstehen Sie?"

The student nodded.

She thought of her husband Joe. United States. An executive family had advertised for a nanny in an Austrian newspaper. She'd met Joe, dainty moustache and holed jeans, in a downtown bar. Rockaby days and Big Nothings. Joe liked living with foreign women who spoke English as though it were an heroic language.

Sunday morning lying in bed, they crossed possibilities via complicated silences.

"Will you marry me?" she asked.

"He moved his arm towards the wall. Shadow-played. A cat, a rabbit. "Yes," he said.

A simple wedding. Two witnesses off the street, and a registrar loudly proclaiming the sanctity of children, church, kitchen.

The following morning. Joe had got out of bed, and straight to the bread-bin. It was empty.

"A nightmare," she'd explained. "I got up while you were sleeping and ate the last slice."

"Damn!" Joe had stamped his foot, and she, still in her dressing-gown, had grabbed the purse and rushed out to the delicatessen.

The man behind the counter had reached to the bottom shelf and brought out a white loaf. She had pinched it with her thumb and forefinger. "It's stale," she'd said.

The man had looked at her with murder in his eyes, and started talking about love thy neighbour and thou shall and shall not.

"Do you realise," she told Joe afterwards, "that people are mad here?"

"Ich möchte Tee und Brot."

Miracle - a mistake-free sentence. She encouraged him to an ingenious touch: he must surely be capable of linking butter with bread and thus form the compound noun "Butterbrot".

She brushed the edge of her right hand along her outstretched left palm.

He looked puzzled.

She repeated the movement, then realised that it was rather inadequate since it would only elicit the verb "to spread" which was not what she wanted.

Nonetheless, tenderly, he raised his hand, and let it come down on his left palm.

She remembered his wish to become a sergeant.

Right, left, under cover! Advance into position A-D-Zero!

That day Joe was called up for service in Vietnam. The cheers, the waves, the noisy "Bon Voyage!"

Months later searching the tree, the grass, the sky.

"Remember the snow, honey?" Joe's hand had zigzagged across the crumpled page. "In this place the blind lead the blind, and some blow their heads off."

No military honours for a coward who had gone insane.

(Joe, love - remember the United States stars, coming out all huge and dazzling, and falling, one by one, into your hands?)

He had chosen a day of pouring rain, the commanding officer told her. Shot his brains out while everyone had breakfast. (If you can call it breakfast with mosquitoes doing the work of surgeons.)

Joe, my love, the snowflakes fell on the sidewalk. I opened my mouth. I tilted my head back. The slivers of snow fell on my tongue. A man with a fur collar stepped in front of me. I heard him say that underneath the snow the grass was green, and how about it, doll?

I threw my head back. The snowflakes fell deeper into my throat. Was it Israel you mentioned once, where burying the dead would have been a useful job?

My coat slipped to the ground.

The last time. Calling the lesson "personal assessment".

She moved the chair closer to his sofa and looked into his eyes.

Journey into his past. In particular his opinion of it.

It transpired that it was neither strong nor clear. The latter due to the fact that even after several lessons his command of the language was still limited.

She motioned him to kneel.

Seeing herself reflected in his pupils, she launched into a symbolic tale. Two beggars standing at opposite ends of a long road.

She mimicked her part by getting up, hunching her shoulders and using the ash-tray as a bowl of alms.

She asked him to do the same, but he declined.

She closed her eyes, and stepped towards him. "Bitte!" - please. Her knees trembled. At convent school the priest's mellow thumb had drawn the ash-cross on her forehead. "Your name, child?" She'd clenched her fist. "Miriam." "That is a Jewish name. What faith has your father?" She'd breathed deeply. "Jewish. But my mother is a Catholic."

The priest had stared at her. So she'd pinched his purple sleeve, remembering that in his sermon he'd said that purple was the colour of mercy.

But he'd wrenched himself free. "Let go, child! God will punish you."

Golden tabernacle. Her hand at the altar-rail, falling. She'd thought of the world's mysteries. God, the ocean, those sparrows caught in brilliant sunlight behind the stained glass window. The church was dynamically still, as all the children got up to receive absolution.

In the name of the Father, the Son, and the - "Tot!" She'd screamed. Wiping the ash-cross from her forehead, and raising her fist in the air - " Er ist tot!"

She opened her eyes. Where the student had been kneeling, there was only the carpet.

Twenty past two. He has never been this late.

She paces the room. Suddenly, footsteps. At her door they pause.

She listens for the familiar tap on the letter-slot. It happens. Then there is a second tap. With a start she realises the slot has been lifted and, with the minimum of noise, been pushed back into place.

The footsteps recede, hurriedly, down the stairs.

On the mat she finds a sheet ripped from a note-pad. It begins with "I" and ends with his name - "Jamie".

She stares at the words in between. " . . . won't be able to continue with the lessons any longer, but do appreciate your trouble."

In the kitchen there are fuchsias in a window-box. They have not been pruned for years, and climb, in conquest of that elusive sun.

What can she expect? He knows the genders and the four cases, and is now able to read the captions to nude pictures in German magazines.

His "Ich verstehe" - "I understand" was just a clinical response.

She lifts the lid of the breadbin. A last slice. She butters it and cuts it into "soldiers".

The view beyond the fuchsias is of a grey drainpipe. She thinks of a rope, the word "hanged" swinging between past and present.

Britain, where things are civilised.

With the edge of her right hand she brushes dead blossoms into her left palm.

On her ageing skin they reveal their inner voice, while staying purely external.

Christine McNeill

LOCHAR PUBLISHING - SPRING TITLES 1991

John Buchan - A History of the First World War ISBN: 0-948403-53-5 Publication: 28 Mar £16

This vivid and authoritative account of the Great War is abridged by the military historian, Victor Neuburg. Illustrated in colour with paintings by official war artists.

Ancient Scotland - Stewart Ross ISBN: 0-948403-54-3 Publication: 28 Mar £16

In a sweeping survey, the author presents and illustrates the history of Scotland's ancient races and relics of their civilizations. Completes a trilogy on Scottish history for Stewart Ross.

The Story of Scotland - Nigel Tranter ISBN: 0-948403-56-X Publication: 28 Mar £ 6.99

The first paperback of this popular illustrated history - an enthralling and turbulent story told not merely in terms of documentary evidence but also revealing the legends and myths.

Rob Roy MacGregor - Nigel Tranter ISBN: 0-948403-75-6 Publication: 28 Mar £ 5.99

In this paperback, Nigel Tranter breathes life into this legendary figure, who whether hero, lovable rogue or outlaw, will never be forgotten in Scotland.

Iona-A History of the Island - F. Marian McNeill ISBN: 0-948403-63-2 Publication: 25 Apr £14.99

Fully revised and updated this is a classic history of and guide to an island whose enchantment is acknowledged worldwide. Including a map of the island and lavish colour photographs.

David Gill

PORTUGUESE POEMS

LETTER TO A YOUNG PORTUGUESE

It's spring - and you'd rather be off to Guincho Beach,
to skim among the green Atlantic breakers,
wetsuit-walking the tightrope of the foam,
or sprawl beside the prostrate topless girls.
But here you are, confined to barracks, morose,
and pondering Portugal, your dark eyes even darker
with that old-fashioned sadness your peers affect
to despise. The editorials have got you down.
The shrinkage of the nation's greatness is like
the clothes that leave your wrists grotesquely bare,
and tighten on your chest. On city squares,
beneath the huge bronze horsemen, you seem to share
the slightly daft democracy of pigeons.
You feel reduced. The sailors in the bars
behind the Torre de Belém have nothing
to discover: the world is mapped, not up for grabs.
And history chains the spirit to that bollard tower,
the long regret, a gradual ebbing of
the tide, sucking at stones and unsteadying feet.
A pity you don't select your heroes better.
Why waste your grief on spoilt Sebastian,
who sank his army in Moroccan sand?
This folly the nation mostly forgave him,
forgives him still, awaiting some new twist
to the national myth. But living in the past
is not for you. Just trust your mistrust of *fado*,
whose singers, with clenched eyes, evoke a past
of spent romance, bringing tears to older cheeks.
It's smallness that bugs you. A small nation, the tail
of Europe . . . Yes, it's true that Spain's not small,
so painfully adjacent, true that France
is big with nuclear reactors, Germany
so rich, and Britain empire-proud at heart.
Yes, Portugal is small. No harm in that.
Small boats, well caulked, will keep the water out.
The signs are good. At dawn the fireworks burst
in festive puffs of smoke above the towns.
The low and leaden clouds of Salazar
have rolled away. A new society
unpacks its long-moist wings. New energies
are loose . . . You shrug your shoulders hopelessly.

It's astrophysics or nothing. Poor Portugal
stares into space with only a poet's eyes.
Not good enough for you. No astronauts
to pilot from Belêm space-caravels
through cosmic seas to quays among the stars.
Flash Gordon beckons from a gantry on the cape
where rockets fizzle and smoke like Roman Candles,
while you sit brooding with broken astrolabe.

The agenda-setters have much to answer for.
Last week the Daily News invited Youth
to write on 'Futility'. A winner! How it appealed!

On pointlessness the young discoursed with passion,
soul-brothers and sisters of Miguel Rovisco
who won all the literary prizes by twenty-eight,
and then, one abject October day,
at Belêm, where da Gama and his men set sail,
discarded his life, his talent and futility
beneath a train. And but for the grace of God,
or the human grace of common sense, they too
might have cracked up. Being young is hard, and yet
the challenge of how to be a Portuguese
is of human proportions. The poverty is not
of Africa or India - a continent,
but a local refuse-tip to be bulldozed flat
with a little political will. You have a gift
for living close together in community,
from which who knows what forms of unexploited
work may spring. Nor do you need to ape
the nuclear wastrels of the high-tech age
and hanker after hideous energy.
Look at the sun you share with Africa!
Look at the waves that beat against your coasts!
-Feel the winds that rounded your forebears' sails,
and swung the windmills of your southern hills.
What discoveries and inventions can be made
to match the needs of an unpretentious people,
and problems solved within your boundaries
may offer hope to Europe when she reels
from yet another nuclear misadventure.
Forget, young friend, the stars, the space-Sebastians.
Forget the big, for they create big problems.
Pursue the small, the relevant, the human.
Look, beneath the moon the windmills spur
their dynamos. Beneath the sun the panels
glow. Unceasing the mountain streams that spin
the turbines in the coombs. And brighter songs
than *fado* rise from spirited guitars.

AZULEJOS

Not prisoners in the bathroom,
but given the license
of the outside walls,
they're extravagant,
rhetorical, repeating
the myths of the people.

Ah, what myths
in this chaste blue world of tiles,
where cool cerulean Mary floats
on pale blue cushions of cloud,
where sky-blue mariners
with astrolabes
go aboard blue caravels
to make the haziest discoveries
in the farthest blue square
of this graph-paper world.

ALENTEJO PLATES

Heavy they are. When you hold one in your hands
you hold the clay, you hold the anchored oak,
the slow routine of a shepherd's day.
You hold the stillness of the Alentejo plain
that sinks beneath a terracotta sun
to heavy night, awaiting rain.

The potters are of this place. Around their kilns
the cowbells chuckle, the egrets saunter,
and snuffling pigs grub up their acorns,
and women in black trilbies fetch the water
from the well, where sunflowers
like Byzantine saints stare down
upon the changeless scene.

We have our feet in clay. There's no refinement here,
no fineness, nothing Japanese. Indeed,
from underneath the plates are terracotta raw
with only the artist's name scratched in.
But turn them over and the patterns blaze,
blue lilies, yellow sunflowers beneath the glaze,
or shots of peasant life: among grey dolmens
a shepherd with his crook and spotted dog,
a farmer and his wife killing the family hog,
and others stripping bark from cork-oaks
leaving dark red arteries of trunks.

Such is the life we buy to hang on our walls,
the simpler past, the labour and the hungry hours,
a sunset the only cinema,
at night the glamour of shooting-stars.
Wired-up and mechanised, our food, our kicks
at second-hand, we need these solid plates
with crude bright pictures as ballast
to keep us steady. They hang
in the bedrooms of memory
recalling those who further up the line
under terracotta suns
fed swine.

CEMITERIO DOS PRAZERES

The City of the Dead I pass by daily.
It has no suburbs. You are either there
or not. It is a perfect city
for those who are there: marble dwellings,
cypress aisles and festive flowers,
a posthumous view of the river.
And always, in the valley between the dead
and the quick (where I pass by daily)
a company of pigeons perpetually circles
like a dark shadow cast by a cloud
turning to glitter of snowflakes,
as if all the souls of the cemetery
had banded together as equals
and were flying in breathless patterns
of unanimous pleasure.

PARROT

Tumult in the street:
it's the teenagers talking their heads off again.
It took me time to realise
that it wasn't plural
but the singular parrot next door.

He's a green Brazilian parrot
with the gift of tongues,
and all his balcony's a stage.
He's never a soliloquy.
He's a whole crowd turning nasty.
He's a hotbed and a butt of abuse.

He's Mussolini at his window
haranguing the fascist mob.
He's the mob screaming back.
His schizophrenic head is reeling with voices
and they all speak at once.
A pentecostal parrot,
what madness,
what talent!

But let him once catch your eye
and he hangs his head,
falls silent,
demure.

The crowds disperse quietly.

WINDMILLS

for Dr Virgílio Borges

Like heavy guns intractable against the sky,
on hill after hill they stand pointing their poles
at grey invasions from the sea.
No more do their full arms fly,
but wind and time,
wind and time,
pass them by.

In gardens all along the coast a newer race
of slender metal mills like giant daisies
stand rusting in the Atlantic breeze,
each with a broken face,
for wind and time,
wind and time
have left their scar.

So what remains for paid-off servants of the wind
is stance, tradition and the picturesque,
unless their chance comes round again
and deftly redesigned,
in wind and time,
wind and time,
they turn the sky.

Note: Dr Borges, active in the field of alternative energy, has invented a
horizontal windmill inspired by the ventilators he observed on Zurich trams.

David Gill

Ken Morrice

SINNER

Gambling was unlawful I was told,
a ploy of Satan's. So it was
for me one Sunday afternoon,
on parole from Sunday school,
sprung free but prisoned tightly still
in Sunday suit, well-polished shoes,
kept specially for that special day -
heavy with sermons, hymns and sins.

By chance I fall among the ungodly,
(overlooked by a feckless lookout)
a solemn solitary boy happening
among them, excited by their laughter,
oaths and cries, the rattle of dice
and flash of coins in pagan sun.
And so trespassing on the edge of town
I join a Babel of money-changers.

Crown & Anchor, Pitch & Toss
engulf me. I stand wide-eyed, entranced,
before (breathless, sinless, an onlooker only)
I climb the hill beyond temptation,
beyond these shiftless, thriftless folk
who break the Sabbath day.

And I feel safe and virtuous until
(not thrust in Sunday School collection box
where they belong) I find the guilty pennies
hot and heavy in my hand.

OLD TORRY

Timeless, you might think, the huddle
of white cottages below the hill
leaning over wooden wharf - an ancestry
and heritage sure of our protection.

But history crumbles at the press of time.
And anyway it was all too personal,
too parochial. The boom of oil
calls louder than the cry of conservation.

Who listens to fuss about tumbledown
old hovels? The jetty too looked dangerous.
Space was needed, steel and concrete
to moor the ships, support the storage tanks.

Yet when summer comes, I see again
the old kirk, the corner sweetie-shop,
the creaking yawls yawing at their ropes.
And at her door a fishwife busy

at her husband's lines, coiled and baited,
careful in their scull. But the cod
and haddock, the red-eyed mackerel,
swim deeper now. Pier looks bleak, empty

of raucous boys quarrelling over their catch
and teasing the gluttonous gulls
that swoop to swallow the wide world.

Not in stones now stands the fisher-town,
in memory only, in old men's minds.

GULLS AT HACKLEY BAY

This year Spring comes early.
Blue skies lead us to the crooked harbour,
past a straggle of white cottages
and fishing-cobbles, still wintering,
cockled on the shore. We mount the cliff
breathless into a sudden gale.

High on moor-top the marram-grass
lies low and frantic sky-larks
decide to fly backwards. Only gulls,
deft harnessers of air, careen effortlessly
across slabs and pinnacles of rock
to skim the creamy sea.

Above deep curve of bay
we watch surf mimic its contours
in endless arcs of white.
Three-score slatted wooden steps
pitch steeply to wet mirror of sand,
an iridescence full of tumbled sky.

We return, awash in golden light,
free-wheeling on the wind, to meet a native
snugly seated in his cliff-top hollow.
He surveys us. "Grand day," says he,
swift to add with dire relish,
"But mind, we'll pay for it later!"

On this bare knuckle of coast,
joy is an intruder.

Ken Morrice

High Risk Tenement

Mary McCabe

Top Right:

Original panelling, brass handles which still turn, dented snibs which still snib. To the right, the kitchen, black range with gas taps, press with plates, swan-necked wooden sink. Curtained bed-recess. To the left, the room. Floral yellow wallpaper, worn red mat. Recess with Jenny''s wardrobe. Above the dressing table, china ducks fly towards the bow window; opposite is the fifties' fawn fireplace with the coal-effect electric fire. Near the window is a built-in display cabinet with willow-pattern plates, Delft china clogs, a Dresden dancer. At the window Jenny peered over the wire curtain rail.

"Here she comes, Miss O'Flaherty. Whit's this she's oan? Pair sowel, I doot she's got it oot a jumble sale. Aw thon prayin - whit's she goat tae show fur it? . . . An here's Fanny Allen, decked oot like a Christmas tree, skirt half up her backside. Yet another fancy man. Dirty dog. Honest tae God, whit a wey tae bring up lassies."

"There's the Pakistanis pittin up their shutters already. Used tae be open aw hoors. Doot they're gettin lazy an Scottified. Wantin their telly at night like everybody else."

One up, Right:

Plate steel on the door, shutters on the windows. Darkness in the air and rubble on the floor. The patches of streetlighting that pass through the holes in the shutters show graffiti on the walls of the ruined front room.

In the kitchen, a hole where the range was now houses rustling nests. The shelves are out of the press, and in the recess are sticky crisp packets.

Top Left:

Kitchen units in avocado, stainless steel sink, lowered ceiling with polystyrene tiles. Black vinyl suite, lamps with metal shades. In the recess, yellow formica table and chairs. Cassette recorder blaring.

"Gonny you shut up that racket?" said Michelle. "Ah've goat French words tae learn fur the morra."

"Efter 'Simple Minds'," promised Karen.

"Wish she'd hurry hersel," moaned Michelle. "She's goat tae ask me aw thae words."

The front door opened and closed. The kitchen door opened and a strange man looked in.

"Heh, Raquel! Thurr two lassies in here."

"Aye. Jist shut the door an come ben. They'll no bother us."

"Mighta known," grumbled Michelle.

"Wull Ah ask ye yer French?"

"Uch, you wullny be able tae."

"Gie's it." Karen took the book. "La . . . fawteel."

"The armchair. Look, you say the English an Ah'll say the French."

"Okay, well, um . . . the bed."

"*Le lit.*"

"Wrang."

"Whit? Ur ye shair?"

"It's 'litt'."

"That's the same thing, ye eedjit!"

"Is it? Goad, it's a funny language."

"Don't swerr at your age. 'Sno nice."

"Blackboard."

"Le tableau noir."

"Right, Ah think. Here, see fur yersel."

"Ah wis wrang! It's *la* tableau noir!"

"Uch, Ah didny think thon wee bit mattered."

"It matters." Michelle looked in despair at the door. "Wish she'd be dane wi it and chuck 'im oot."

One Up, Left:

Andrew poked for a while before he saw that it was in fact the key to his daughter's house. His own key had red masking tape on it. At the fourth attempt it fitted. Without taking his coat off and hanging it on the back of the door he turned left into the kitchen and put the light on. Dirty milk bottle and his bag of Forfar bridies on the table. Ashes on the hearth and Friday's dishes in the sink. Original sash window, two casements cracked.

He switched on the electric fire and slumped into an armchair pitted with cigarette burns. He felt in his coat pocket. As he drew out the bottle and raised it to his lips, the cigarette in his other hand dangled closer to the chair arm.

Middle Left:

Scribbles on the walls, dartboard on the door. Nappies on the fireguard, a football on the shelf of the alcove beside the bow window. Low polystyrene ceiling, no ornaments. Sideboard with a panel smashed in, couch with a slash in the back of it, crossed bayonets on the same wall where, through the ceiling and across the landing, Jenny keeps her wild ducks.

"Whit'll we dae, but, if he shows?" whimpered Angie.

"He'll no show."

"But whit if he does?"

"He'll be pickin his teeth oot the backie his neck."

"But . . ."

"Fur Chrissake wumman!" Ronnie's roar set the wean howling. "Thoan pizent dwaarf'd nae mair show his dial nor fly in the air. It wis the bevvy talkin!"

"Ooooohhh . . ."

"Um Ah tae freeze tae daith, or whit?"

"Ah'm gettin it fur ye!" Angie scuttled to the kitchen and hauled a black studded jerkin off the pulley. Two doors are missing from the kitchen units, and the washing machine no longer works. A crate of beer stands on top of the fridge, and Angie has been unable to get the stain of Ronnie's Tuesday dinner out of the wallpaper.

Top Right Again:
Jenny cast her eyes over the motorway to the spare ground beyond. The works now gave the sky a reddish tinge. The sailors and the shepherds would be in nightly delight if they stayed where she did.

A group of youths at the corner caught her eye. Spiky, scrubby, studdy, with their eye on the empty house and its lead pipes, sure's fate. "Away hame, boys!" she called out, softly enough that she would not be heard.

Jenny reached for her Zimmer frame and shuffled towards her bed.

Middle Right:
Sketches and watercolours covered the walls. A posy of pansies, Kelvingrove Park in spring, Burns' cottage in winter, Sacred Heart of Jesus. Where Jenny kept her ducks and Ronnie his bayonets, Ella had an upright piano, inlaid with mother-of-pearl, brass candlabras without and an out-of-tune harp within.

Ella awoke with a start. The telly was whistling. She switched it off, sniffed and made for the kitchen. Her cupboards were red and white, and on the walls were little Germanic hearts and baskets hanging with ribbons and dried flowers. The cooker was the old-fashioned sort, without pilot lights, and the gas taps were turned off.

"The electric blanket." She rushed back to the room recess and hauled back the duvet. No problem there. Perhaps the fuse-box? She wandered back to the lobby. Under the front door curled thick smoke.

Ella opened the door. She was met by a dense cloud, a crackling noise, and a red glare on the landing. Quickly she shut the door again. She half-started for the telephone, then stopped, recalling that she had been 'Number Unobtainable' for the past quarter. Who . . . what . . . She had flung open the door again before she remembered that she would have to take a deep breath. A lungful of fumes and "Fire!" bawled into the close.

No response, but the crackling was nearer. She would have to shout again, take in more smoke to her delicate throat. She held her breath, bounded across the landing and pounded on the hot door. Without waiting for a reply she started upstairs, to use Mrs Cope's phone. But what if the fire came from beneath and cut her off? Holy Mother of God. She hurried downstairs again. But what about poor Mrs Cope up the stair, crippled and maybe soon to be burnt? She started up again. But Mrs Cope would never answer the door at that time of night anyway. The fire brigade? She started down again. But the phone box on the corner was permanently vandalised. What about that dame across the landing from Mrs Cope? Would she not have a phone? Yes, she would have a phone. As Ella began the ascent once again the crackles grew louder, the smoke stung her eyes and blotted everything from view, and she felt the searing heat. She screamed, and her throat choked.

Top Left Again:
"Get the brigade!" croaked Ella. "The place is ablaze!"

"Ah'll get ma mammy!" Michelle tried the handle of the room door. The snib was on. She battered at it. "Heh, Mum!"

Margaret took her time getting to the door. She wore a dressing gown with nothing underneath. "Whit's up?"

"The hoose is on fire."

64

By the light of the bedside lamp Michelle saw the man struggling into his trousers. She had never seen a bare man before.

"Oot the wey! Raquel! Lemme by!" The man pushed past Margaret and Ella and thundered down the stairs.

"He's left his simmit," observed Michelle.

"Dial 999!" wailed Ella.

"Find ma slippers!" barked Margaret at the girls as she picked up the phone. "Naw, don't. Jist get oot tae the street."

Top Right Again:

Bang, bang, bang. Jenny shivered and pulled the covers over her head. "Whozzat? Botherin me at ma ain door." Bang! "If it's no the bad men fae next-door it's the scruff fae the middle landin. Whit a life!" Bang! Bang! A tear rolled down her cheek. "Scram!" she called, too softly to be heard. If they banged again she would phone her son. Or the police.

Bang! "Mrs Cope! Are you there?" Sounded like her next-door. "Mrs Cope! The place is on fire!"

Jenny put on her bedside lamp and flung off the blankets. Her clothes were over the chair and her Zimmer stood by the bed. She crawled in pain to the chair, but before she could dress the light went out. In the dark she found her Zimmer, stumbled to the kitchen door and opened it. Dense black smoke drove her back. Before she could shut the door the kitchen was thick with it. She dropped to her knees, lost her Zimmer, scrabbled for it, crawled in blind panic away from the smoke. Choking and spluttering, she charged head-first into the wall, felt upwards and found the hooks of the window-sash. She pushed in vain: the window was snibbed against the bad folk outside. Her left hand still trailed the Zimmer, and with her last surge of adrenalin she stood upright and smashed it through the pane.

In the Street:

"What a carry-on, eh?" Ella folded her arms tightly against the wind.

"Ah knew it!" Margaret wiped her eyes. "Ah sayd thae glue-sniffers wid burn the place doon in the end."

Angie buried her face in Ronnie's shoulder and began to sob quietly.

"I don't know that it was the glue-sniffers," mused Ella.

"How?"

"I go down sometimes to give Mr Macdougall a hand."

"Ye do?"

"With him being on his own, you know. If I cook a meal I take him half."

"Very good of you, Miss O'Flaherty."

"Well, it's the Christian thing to do. Anyway, I've noticed, when he's . . . well, got a drink in him, he sometimes falls asleep with a cigarette in his hand."

"Naw. He widny a been okay if it hud sterted in his hoose."

"I don't know. Just one up, it would have been easy for him to . . ."

"No if he wis stoatin it widny." Margaret broke off as Andrew loomed in view.

"Awfy business, awfy, awfy business." Andrew shook his head. The shock, and the night air had sobered him up.

"We were wondering how it could have started," said Ella.

Andrew lowered his voice. "Ah wouldny be surprised if yon Malik had done it." ˙

"What, deliberately? Burn his own shop?"

"For the insurance! He'd do anything for money, he's that stingy."

"But I couldn't believe that of him. After all, there are children staying . . ." Ella froze in mid-sentence. Insurance. The renewal notice had come with the phone bill and she had not been able to decide which to pay.

"Never gives credit under any circumstances," said Andrew. "No even tae his own neighbours."

The phone had been cut off. That must mean that she . . . mustn't it?

"I hope Mrs Cope's no too bad." There was no response. "I'm sayin, I hope Mrs Cope's not too bad."

"I hope so. She was lucky they got her out before the fire reached her flat."

"They do say it's the smoke that's the real killer," said Andrew.

Angie's window exploded and everyone jumped back.

"If it wis Heggie," growled Ronnie, "Ah'll smash his bloody skull in fur him. But Ah still think he widny hae the guts."

"Ah know him," sobbed Angie, "Ah wis merrit tae him. An Ah tell ye he wid huv the guts."

"Well, if he did huv the guts, he'll no huv them fur lang. He'll be wearin them roon his knees fur bloody garters, so he wull."

The four-year-old grinned, and wiped his nose on the sleeve of the six-year-old, who was carrying the baby in her arms.

Ella's window exploded. "My drawings!" she cried. "A lifetime's work."

"Miss O'Flaherty," Michelle edged in closer. "Did you go tae Art School?"

"In my day there wasn't money for such things!"

"That's whit Ah want tae dae when Ah leave. Go tae Art School."

"Ah've saw that wumman drawin hur picturs," Karen confided in a whisper to her sister. "They're a just copied affa postcairds!"

"My work has gone all over the world," announced Ella. "I've been paid £100 for a single painting, many's the time."

"Gonny let me see yer pictures sometime?"

"If there's any left after all this."

"It's aw the wee nice things, intit?" said Margaret. "Aw the wee memories. Photies o ma lassies when they were weans. Nae insurance is gonny replace that."

Surely. She had had the money to pay one of them. It was just both, coming at once, and at a bad time of year, with heating bills and . . . but her phone had been cut off. So . . . but why could she not remember doing it? Surely she had paid one of them, she did have the money for that, she had planned to.

Margaret's window burst.

"If wee Heggie hud onythin tae dae wi aw this," swore Ronnie, "onythin at aw . . . Ah'll knock him intae orbit. He'll be wan o thae stars lookin doon at us when Ah've finished wi him. Correction - he'll be aw o thae stars."

Mary McCabe

Judy Steel

THE SOLSTICE STONE

Dismembering the Eden of dead apple trees
On midsummer's day
I uncovered a sunburst of stone
Amongst the swinecress fronds.
What mason's hands
With gnarls and scars to match the apple's bark
Gouged out with careful chisel these' worn radials?
What Aikwood laird instructed him
In the embellishment of a new-born tower?
In the midge-laden dusk
My mind creates the donors
Of my solstice gift.

VIDEY ISLAND, REYKJAVIK

Shadows stretch from silhouettes
Against the midnight sun,
And old Johanne lies at last
Happed in a blanket of cloud-coloured pansies
And the crisp white marble sheet
Of the bed she sought langsyne.

When the shroud has fragmented
And the flesh decayed
From her arthritic, brittle bones,
They will be enfolded again in the husband's embrace
Six decades awaiting her here;
And the dust of Magnus and Byorny
Will return again to the dead womb that long ago
Sanctioned their short lives.

How did you mark time, Johanne,
For those sixty shorn years?
Who planted the pansies, strewed today's fresh flowers,
And commissioned the sungilded testament
To your reunion?

BENIGN INVASION

It's a russet day:
The air hangs between damp and beaded mist;
A pheasant whirs from tangled branches,
And the tower is ripe with her mysteries.

The oak door swings inwards.
Snaking up the kerry-handed staircase
Run rubber-soled invaders.
Unhardened fingers caress old crevices,
Trace the names scratched in crumbled plaster
Of farmhand, lover, prisoner of war.

Old chaff lies sterile in the stone flagged floor:
A legacy of harvests reaped and threshed
by long-dead holders of the pencilled names.
Now other seeds germinate
And in her many-chambered womb
The tower feeds the embryos of imagination.

Such a day casts no shadows.
Tower-captivated, the invaders sit
Cross-legged on cobbles, bielded by stone walls,
Telling new tales of old and unknown times:
They mark their futures out beside the past
And leave their names etched on the plaster page.

FOR NICOLE BOULANGER

Who was born in the same year as my daughter,
and who died in the Lockerbie air disaster of 1988.

I saw your drizzle-dampened photograph
Smiling amongst the banks of formal flowers;
I heard your mother's words of love and grief -
And all at once the horror of that night
Distilled into one loss, one death, one waste.

You died amongst these rolling Border hills:
The same our daughters played and rode and walked in -
They make a nursery fit to shape and mould
A spirit swift as water, free as air.

But you, west-winging through the Christmas dark
Found them no playground but a mortuary -
Your young life poised for flight to woman's years
Destroyed as wantonly as moorland game.

The men and women of the stricken town
Receive you reverently into their care:
Blood-sister to the daughters nurtured here,
Your shrine is granite, grass, and unsought peace.

Judy Steel

Uilleam Neill

COILLE GHILLESBAIG

Di-Luain soilleir is mise a'coiseachd
bho Drochaid Luachair gu ruig Loch Dubh
fo sgàil na coille is ri taobh na h-aibhne,
feur ùr a fàs air gach innis rèidh;
fèath anns an iarmailt, is air na linntean:
mo shaoghal boidheach fo chiùineas glan,
mo shùil gu tric air na meallan crùnta
le boillsgeadh deireannach an tìde chaidh.

An eala bhàn is a leannan dìleas
air sgàthan uisge bu mhìne gnè:
gealagan-làir air na bruachan sìnte
is lus-a-chrom-chinn a' tighinn gu blàth.
Se duine coibhneil a th'ann, 'illesbaig
nach marbh creutair air bith son spòrs:
gach eun is ainmhidh a rèir a rian
is mi maraon leis an domhan gu lèir.

Nam sheasamh tosdach an cridhe na coille
faidhbile is darach is iubhar is fhailm,
a dh'fhàs gu ìre iomadh bliadhna romham
gun leòn air bun ac' bho sàbh no tuath,
tha mi an dòchas gum bi iad a smèideadh
an geugan uaisle gu h-àrd san speur
fad iomadh bliadhna os cionn Ghillespaig
a shàbhail beò caoirean binn nan craobh.

GILLESPIES WOOD

Bright Monday and me walking/ from the Bridge of Rushes to the Black Loch/ under the shadow of the wood by the riverside/ fresh grass growing in each level clearing/ calm in the heavens and on the river pools/ my bonny world under a pure peace/ my eye often on the round hills crowned/ with the last gleam of the season that's gone.

The white swan and her faithful lover/ on the most smooth mirror of water/ snowdrops spread out on the banks/ and daffodils coming to bloom./ A kind man is Gillespie/ who will not kill any creature for sport/ each bird and beast in its own way/ and me as one with the whole of creation.

Standing quiet in the heart of the wood/ beech and oak and yew and elm/ that came to full growth many a year before me/ with no wound on the trunk from saw or axe./ I hope that they will be waving/ their noble branches high in the heavens/ for many a year over the head of Gillespie/ who saved the sweet murmur of the living woodland.

TRIUR BHANA-BHUIDSEACH

When shall we three meet again?
Ghoid me eachdraidh as an ceann
is chuir mi eachdraidh briagach ann.

Chuir mi na maithean ac' gu deas
is air an comhairle rinn mi sgrìos.

Chuir mi 'n ionmhas mòr fo smachd
is thuirt mi riù gu robh iad bochd.

Cuin a bhios sinn ann nar triùir?
Coma leinn is sinn gun aobhar.

THREE WITCHES

When shall we three meet again?
I stole history from their heads/ and put lying history in its place.
I sent their great ones south/ and destroyed their assembly.
I put their great wealth under subjection/ then told them they were poor.
When shall we three meet again?/ Never mind, there's no need.

TAIGH-TASGAIDH

Cha robh *Beitidh Burke* cho boidheach idir
an deidh iomadh bliadha air mhisg,
thall thairis an Roimh,
an droch bhargan a bh'ann

Ach co a th'againn an seo . . .
am Bùidsear 'sa chota dearg
a' coimhead oirnn le sùil bheag phriobach
is e cho tapaidh gun d'thug e dhuinn
righrean nach gabhadh ri
scribble, scribble, scribble,
boets and bainters.

Anns a Chathair Phroiseil
coig mile air falbh oirnn,
is mòr aca fhein
gu bheil an cuid Bheurla
coimhlionta, glan, ceart,
as fheàrr san dùthaich, their iad.

Taobh a muigh air a mhòintich
am measg thom chnàimh
cluinnidh tu gairm Iain Ruaidh
is gaoth a' cathadh nan sìon.

MUSEUM

Betty Burke was not so bonny at all/ after the many years of boozing/ over yonder in Rome./ A bad bargain he was.

But who do we have here . . ./ The Butcher in his red coat/ watching us with a little twinkling eye/ and he so clever to give us/ kings who would have nothing to do with those who "scribble, scribble, scribble"/ "boets and bainters".

In the Proud City/ five miles away from here/ they think much of the fact/ that their share of English is/ accomplished, pure, correct,/ the best in the country, they say.

Outside on the moor/ among the mounds of bones/ you will hear the cry of John Roy (Stuart)/ and the wind blowing the rain.

Charles Edward Stuart was so called when escaping dressed as a servant lass.

CUMHAICHD NAM BARD

Ged a bha sleaghan fada aca
is fèithean cho làidir ris na seichean
a chòmhdaich an targaidean,
ged a bha danarrachd leòghain
air gach fear dhiubh,
aig na curaidhean a dhoirt am fuil
air talamh an athardha
an glaodhan dearga casgraidh,
cha robh ni air fhaigail ach tosd.

Ach an sàmhchair chlabhstar
tha sgoilearan sìothchail a leughadh
dà shreath coimhliont a seinneas
tre ceò domhain nan ceud:

*Thoiribh an naigheachd, a choigrich, gu ruig Lacedaimon:
ḡur umhail don aithntean, tha sinne nar laighe an seo.*

Is a dh'ainneòin bàis is tìm
Chaneil iad gu leir gun ghairm.

THE POWER OF POETS

Though they had long spears/ and sinews as tough as the hide/ that dressed their shields/ though the boldness of lions/ was on every man of them/ to the warriors who spilled their blood on their native soil/ in the red noise of battle/ nothing remained but silence.

But in quiet cloisters/ peaceful scholars read/ two polished lines that sing/ through the thick mist of centuries:

Stranger, bear news to the Spartans/ that here we lie obedient to their commands.

And despite death and time/ they are not lacking a cry.

AN TOBAR

Cha robh fìos agam air mo cheud thadhal
gu robh an tobar sin cho domhainn.
Gu suilbhir leig mi sios an ròpa,
ag iarraidh meise dhen uisge slàn.

Ged nach robh agam ròp bu laidire
shnìomh mi snaithlean a bu thighe ann
gus an danaig comas tarruing suas dhomh,
cuinneag a bha gu bhith làn.

Bha feadhainn ann a thug dhomh cobhair
le iasad bucaid agus ròpa buan.
Glan is soilleir as an fhuaran slàinteil
dh'olainn balgam à cùpan fionnar.

Air là brònach thanaig gràisg oirnn
le cridhe crìonta is ceann ro-chruaidh,
dh'òl iad an làn-shàth bho Allt na Miodail,
is chuir sin gamhlas mòr nam broinn.

Thilg iad salachar nar tobar fìorghlan
o nach bu toigh leò ar fuaran slèibhe,
ach thig soilleireachd air ar bùrn a rithist
is òlaidh sinne nuair a bhios e rèidh.

THE WELL

I did not know on my first visit/ that the well was so deep./ Cheerfully I let down the rope,/ seeking a vessel of clean water.

Though my rope was not very strong/ I wove other strands into it/ until I was able to draw up/ a pail that was nearly full.

There were some who helped me/ with the loan of ropes and buckets./ Clean and bright from the spring/ I would drink a mouthful of clear water.

On a sad day there came down on us a mob/ with withered heart and hard head,/ who had drunk their fill at the Stream of Flattery/ and that filled their bellies with spite.

They threw dirt into our crystal well,/ since they did not like our moorland spring./ But the water will clear yet/ and a generation drink when it settles.

William Neill

W N Herbert

SNY (in Beckley)

I thi oor afore thi voices cum
lyk midgis tae this plum

pub gairden whaur
evenin leans upo thi bar,

trees' anguls hintin at
thi tilt o licht's hat,

we sit and read o thi amorous mime
twa slugs perform wi a baa o thir slime

and an unnamed burd o prey
laives uts creh inna fruit-tree's splay.

An then thi weel-heelt puntirs came:
Eh caucht masel bleezin, assignin blame

no tae thir accents but
til these stevins' vacant note,   (voices)

an kent ut still a dispersonin scheme
tae faa back here oanna Scoattish dreme.

Thir bairns rise lyk eisenin gulls   (desirous)
til th'intermittent pulse

o ripe plums faain, thon dirdin clyte   (resounding rap)
o purpie fruct aa reekt in white

that waukens us fae time
as tho thi stars geed a bluey skime

afore they sklytit doon,   (fell heavily)
an space's outh wiz beamfu wi this tune   (outermost parts)

that pangs a keelie's thrappil   (hawk's throat)
an fills thi wurm that pangs thi appil   (packs)

an fills yir een wi gloamin
as licht gaes thru thi fruit-trees' strummin.

SYTHE

Thi swift
      that draps
frae thi nest intac flicht
wull fleh owre thi taps
o thi dey an thi nicht
fehv thoosan mile

wull hear uts skryle
while three year
wull pass inna breer   (sprint)
nor wull ut rest
till ut biggs uts ain nest
this Eh attest:

Guidbye.
        Livan oan
thi ootside o thi sky
or wi you by
isnae much o a choice
gin yi waant ma voice
no tae mell wi yir ain
lyk saalt waatir wi rain
gin yi waant me tae heal
skaiths Eh can't feel   (hurts)
gin yi waant me tae grow
or jist go:

Snow
        wull bandage thi groond
whaur therr's nae wound
thi buried wurd
wull live withoot soond
withooten wan burd
thi sky is attuned.
Whaur Eh land
nithin is planned
wha Eh mate
is separate.

WHO NEEDS THE SAC?

Within fehv meenuts
o hittan Dundee,

sittan i thi Seagate
scrievan a wee

daithliss wan, Eh
hear a wolf-whissul

frum a passin van
an, lukein up ti see

sum classic haurdman,
get a smack oan thi pow fae 2p . . .

an therr are sum farts
say Dundee disnae suppoart
                        thi arts!

THE MAVIE AS MESSIAEN
(overheard in Dundee bus station)

Nou, believe me or
believe me nut, this
burd cums flehin by
me. Eh dinna ken

whit ut iz, a
thrush orra starlin, an
ut's churpin awa lyk
hell. An Eh sehs

This burd is trehin
tae tell me sumthin:
ut's sat therr churpin
awa lyk bluddy hell.

An Eh gaes ahent
thi bhush, an therr's
a cat, croochan doon.
An Eh sez: You -

get thi eff awa!

SONG

Nivir tell, nivir tell
motives ur wurds
wi aa ken well
but pit thigithir
they mak a spell
that maks us dae
whit wi nivir can tell -

Nivir tell, nivir tell
truth huz a color
truth huz a smell
thae that ken these
nivir dae well
truth issa hoose
whaur nane can dwell -

Nivir tell, nivir tell
yi hear desire
jowe lyk a bell
toll fur thi fair
an toll fur thi fell
gin yi luvc
yi nivir can tell.

W N Herbert

I Was On The Dance Floor When

Ken Cockburn

". . . The nymphs are departed.
And their friends, the loitering heirs of City directors;
Departed, have left no addresses."
TS Eliot *The Waste Land* III, 'The Fire Sermon'

A pile of crates and boxes, some of them sodden underneath from rotted vegetables. I look for the dry ones. For sleeping on, it's not cold but they stop the damp rising. There's a few are all right, I flatten them with my boot. My hands get slime on them, I wipe them on straw, and the smell hits me. A wasp buzzes around my head, loads of flies buzzing around, they settle on whatever they fancy but fly up again whenever I move. I find a couple of allright apples and a melon bad at one end only. Some shrivelled lemons which are probably allright but not much use really. And a newspaper which is recent and untouched by soft fruit except for a small corner which is a soggy yellow. I root around in the rest of the pile but there's nothing else. When I walk on down the road I see my boots have got covered in something and two sparrows are already picking at what I've left. I start on one of the apples.

I was on the dance floor when the boat lurched and the needle of the record scraped across it. I was being dragged down by my clothes. You have to imagine hundreds of half-heads in the water, because they were being dragged down by their clothes. I was very tired. The boat lurched and the needle on the record scraped across it. I couldn't see anyone else. I could hear a scraping noise, a whooshing of water and buzzing in my ears. I was on the dance floor when the boat lurched. I couldn't see anyone else. Many were in their twenties, with glittering careers ahead of them. He had an idea to leave the work he was doing and become a writer. I was very tired.

It was just before dawn I saw the body, from the bridge. I woke up with the cold and went for something to burn, the others were still sleeping. I had a pile of wood under one arm, there's a pub the other side of the river they're doing up, so you get all these old struts dumped in skips outside it, full of nails but allright. The river was right down, and she was on the mud bank, still half in the water. She still had most of her clothes on, maybe that was why she'd been down there for so long. Her head was thrown back, and I could see her face through her hair. It was white and soft-looking, it looked like if you touched it it would just give way. Then I went back and did the fire. I saw her picture in the paper, I mean it must have been the same woman but I couldn't see the resemblance myself. I went back to the bridge during the day, I was crossing it for more wood out the skip but maybe I would have gone anyway, I kept expecting her still to be there. There were people around for a while, police and that but then it was just mud again, and you don't even see it if the river's high.

i could recognise the landmarks. i knew where i was at any one moment, but i could not make connections between one place and another. i would turn a corner and find myself somewhere new, recogniaable certainly, but quite cut off from where i had just been; i could not understand how i had arrived there, and had no means of turning back, of retracing my footsteps. the only faces which acknowledged me looked as baffled as i was; others, who looked familiar, walked past, their thoughts elsewhere. although quite calm, i felt something building inside me - not anger or frustration as such, for it was both more intangible and more intense than that. i sensed i would lose all my present calm if i let this new sensation enter into me. for some reason i began to follow a tramp, a filthy old man carrying plastic bags. every now and then he would stop, to sit on a bench, or a at a bus stop, where he drank from a bottle. finally he left it in a hedge, when it was empty or when he'd had enough.

gradually i began to lose my bearings, as he followed a seemingly haphazard route down streets i did not know, not far from places i knew well, but very much foreign territory. he entered a derelict house and i followed him. the place was filthy, with all sorts of rubbish littering the floor. inside were two other tramps, slouched in the corner of a room beneath a window. i became taken up with the house, which had been quite grand once; the rooms were spacious, and the door-frames and pelmets were intact and still attractive. there was a large dark-wood wardrobe in a corner, and on the opposite wall a single coathanger hung on a hook. the walls had damp and the floor was covered in all sorts of debris, ashes, burst binbags, empty beer cans and bottles. when i looked again at what was happening between the tramps, i saw that an argument had developed. the other two men were rising, using the walls to help themselves up, but they looked hardly capable of standing, let alone brawling. he swore at them but then turned away and slouched out, muttering to himself. he went on muttering all the way to the bridge.

when we reached the bridge i felt constrained to stop. he continued walking, and i watched him move further and further away from me. it was only when i could see clearly that he had reached the opposite embankment that i could bring myself to step onto the bridge. i tried to run, but my legs would not respond; they refused to move any faster than the tramp's slow pace they had fallen in with. however, he had stopped to look over the embankment wall at the mud bank below. the river was very low, and the surface of the mud had dried a little in the sun. i did not remember ever visiting that part of the river, but i felt a terrible nostalgia as i waited for him to end his contemplations. we walked on, until we came to a more industrial area. he turned off between two buildings, the sides of which formed a narrow, high-walled lane, and clambered over a lower wall which sealed it at the end. on the other side was a bizarre little square, enclosed by the wall he had just climbed over and the end walls of three industrial units. two were of corrugated metal, the other of modern patterned red-brick, which looked like a site office rather than a factory or a warehouse. underfoot the ground was part cracked stone, part earth, with weeds sprouting everywhere. there was rubbish here as well, but less than in the house, and a blackened area in

*the middle was covered in ashes and scorched wood, where fires had
burned.*

I arrive when it's getting dark, nobody else is around tonight. I can hear
his radio from behind the wall. No traffic. What I like is the quiet. Useless if
it's raining, only the ledge to sit under but it's good for the quiet. No
disturbances. Except for his metal heels, and the dog going mental at the
bats, what a carry-on. First patrol now. What a doss, walking a fucking
alsatian and listening to the radio all night. But no trouble. Probably can't be
arsed. Makes a change. I break some of the wood that's left with my boot
and make sure I avoid the nails. I found 20p this afternoon so I have a box of
matches and a packet of Rizlas. Use the paper to get the wood going, done
the crossword. Roll up the tobacco from the dogends and light it off the
fire, make the matches last. Save them up and build a model cathedral eh?
Cardboard still allright, the big box is fine. Lie down in the warm. Stink of
burning paint. Rough smoke this, but beggars can't be choosers. The woman
in the river, she's been in and out my head all day, soft face. In a fridge now.
No bevvy. Tight bastards, I should've swiped the fucking bottle.

*his lined, grimy face in the firelight. deep, flickering shadows on the
walls. i begin to smell the place slightly, the burning, the rubbish, his body. an
odd sort of conclusion, if that's what it is, here of all places. i can't think of
them now, but there must be better than this. how did i end up here? perhaps
if i wait until dawn and then go back.*

    - you look cold, dear, sit in a bit closer.

    - what does all this have to do with me?

    - same as it's to do with me. want a draw?

    - thank you. are we connected in some way? am i meant to be here?

    - i thought you would have known. it's the centre.

    - the centre of what?

    - your centre. you walk till you find it.

    - but why here? and why you?

    *- you chose me, i don't know. it doesn't matter anyway, this is it. and
you're here. finished with the fag?*

    - but why here of all places? i don't understand.

    *- if you don't like it, dear, no problem, there's other doors. here and
there. not to be recommended though, you could have a long wait till you
get dreamt again. got a thing about dossers or something?*

    *- no. i never gave them much thought. is this some sort of punishment
for something i've done?*

    *- no, not a punishment. it's like a half clearing out from the last time and
a half preparation for the next time round. so you can go on without being
scared. what was it you were scared of?*

    *- i suppose i was most afraid of being poor. of having to beg. scavenging,
being an alcoholic. i was always frightened of tramps. i couldn't understand
how they could let themselves go like that, how they could give up and stop
fighting. i assumed everyone could choose, and would choose like me. that
was it. and now i have to start all over again, somewhere else. are there any
clues?*

- not really, maybe another river.
- swapping dirty rivers. here is as good a place as any. where would have i been before, i wonder? and you, don't you remember anything?
- sorry.
- what happens now?
- you just wait.
- does it take long?
- all these questions at this stage in the game! i don't know, i'm just like the doorman, i make sure you get in allright but i don't get to see what goes on inside, that's your thing.
- all the faces i knew look like yours now. all the rooms i lived in look like this place. all the days i saw look like this fire, all the nights like the shadows on the walls. and then the river. that frightened me. i was on the dance floor when the boat lurched and the needle on the record scraped across it. days like fire. nights like shadows. i can leave you to your dreams. goodbye.

Not even light. Warm enough though, some heat off the fire yet. Roll over and forget about it. They used to say it was cheese did it, must have been that melon. It's put me right off. Where to? It'll be light soon. See where the feet wander. I wonder if those bastards have got any left, they're always crashing out with half-empty bottles. Half-full. Get there before they get a thirst on them again. And I've still got that apple. I've always maintained the importance of starting the day with a proper breakfast. Item, one apple, red, bruised on one side only. Take them a bit of solid fuel, keep them happy. Right.

Note: The second section ("I was on the dance floor when..." consists of sentences excerpted from newspaper reports of the sinking of the Marchioness *on the Thames in August 1989 with the loss of some 50 lives.*

Ken Cockburn

Donald Adamson

A COLONIAL OFFICER VISITS PERIM

(Perim is an island in the Red Sea, where it joins the Gulf of Aden)

They brought him in the motor launch
from Al Turbah. Heavy keys
opened the long-locked bungalow
and dust choked the room as shutters were thrown back.
The motes danced, then settled. 'Leave me' he said.

He was hungry. Some herdsmen
gave him goat-stew and rice.
The sun was low as he pulled his chair to a balcony
half-filled, waterlogged with sand.
He poured a beer, body-warm,
and slumped back, could have dozed off

when the great liner, India-bound
surprised him, gliding towards him
in a calm intricacy of light. It was close enough
to hear the band playing a quickstep.
His mind filled in the rest:
the tables, the glasses cold enough for rivers to form
at a fingertip, the cream-jacketed stewards,
the ordered universe, deck upon deck -

then it was gone. Only the wake, phosphorescent,
unravelling like wool, betrayed its passing.
Shepherds had lit a fire
against a backdrop of date palms. Moving shapes
threw shadows from a kerosene lamp
and someone sang to a drum.
But later there was silence,
only the night, a warm wind
lapping Perim, crashing onto the land,
breaking slowly, slowly like a wave.

SHAMAN

When our cat was dying
my son said 'Dad
can you write a poem,
one of your kind
that doesn't rhyme?'
This isn't it.

Only regret
not to know
with the rainmaker
and the blesser of corn
where they fell to earth
and wait to be found
the healing words, secret syllables.

BATTLEGROUND

To escape the troubles
they moved out of Belfast -
now they have a chip-shop in Glasgow.

Kids say the daughter smells of chips
(rifling the air behind her, sniffer dogs
whose laughter explodes).

She'll serve the chips each night
and maybe she'll get used to it
as the haggis flies like baton rounds
and chicken grenades
are tossed in the fryer's machine-gun nest.

Through the blasts of her growing
and the moon's lacerations, who will know her,
a life taped, splinter-proof, like glass

with hooded face
to walk among the lipped craters,
weaponless?

BLONDE CHILDREN

I remember the blonde children
with foreign names, streaking like comets
into the class from a sun
of wartime unions.

Dad 'in the army',
'on a whaler . . .'

Something must have flashed through a wire
at their making,
arcing across a bulb, incandescent
for them to be so fair.

Yellow marsh flowers,
they should have wished for them
to keep that light

or fallen among us be
reeds with electric hiss

or bulrushes,
earthbound, spikeleted with stars.

SETTINGS

You rise and cover yourself in a green dress,
hiding deep springs within a valley of grass
that we leave as, ever practical, you scan
the day - you become a bright, searching sun
whose beams are chores, necessities and lists
that parch the grass, disperse the early mist.
So it begins, and after the first coffee
greenness seems a mirage or memory.

We go to shops where mangoes smell of pine,
a resinous forest; but the aubergines
are purple as burnt shadows under bare
desert rocks. May it be circular,
the track that compassless I take, may you
bring down the sun, and with the evening dew
water the earth to greenness; may your setting
be springs that waken us to day's forgetting.

VISION

Today even the rocks feel hot to the touch.
Scotland lies sunning herself
on the deck of her Pre-Cambrian boat.

In her bones she remembers herself as Africa.
Her green dress covers the skeleton
of deserts and coal-forests.

For millions of years she's been sailing
on a tectonic barge, heading northward.
Recently she's discovered man

but she doesn't rate him, she's making a trap for him
out of electric coils of atmosphere
and a cage of oceans.

There will be no more sea.
She'll rise from the waves
Venus of boiling clouds and acid air.

TO MY FATHER, ON THE ANNIVERSARY OF HIS DEATH

We grow older. You
grow away from us as children do
that find the ways of their elders irksome, prefer
their own kind, own company.

WORD-HERDS

Up river
along the banks of the blood-line
my ancestors graze their cattle.

Herders of Scots, Gaelic and Welsh
how could I warn them
of the hard winter ahead,
the word-stock lost, place names
strewn like bones across the map of Scotland?

Donald Adamson

Ranald Macdonald

THE TRANSLATION OF THE TOAD-QUEEN

A toad-queen saw, upon her belly, spots, and counted them:
seven times the number of her years.
The star-singer - he who tutored her in magick -
confirmed they shone in portent and were,
as the liver-line is to he who perceives it
rightly in his palm, a sign of translation.

She changed, upon the moment of the moon
in the arc of the lily-pond, and became
a maiden. A King's son passed and married her.

They said she was a work of the stars,
they said that every time she spoke it was as if
a piece of gold had fallen from her lips.
The sick of the land pressed fingers on her robe,
a small shrine was erected by the pond.
The priests who heard her speak confessed
she seemed to have no history or past.
The poets stretched their lyrics to encompass her
and harped her praise. The old King
spoke of femininity, the Prince
averred her breeding, the Queen remarked
of that one could not tell. But for the rest

they all believed a potent demiurge
had placed her on the earth not long before.

A feast was held to celebrate her birth.
From the white lands and the grey lands,
from the townlands and the kingdoms
near the sun, there came a slow procession.
And at her casement window, looking forth,
the Princess whispered, I have quelled
and quelled again the nature of the toad.
There were underlords and overlords, Kings
and Queens and seneschals and old magicians
speaking out of turn. They dined
on viands stewed in wine, on forest honey,
and sweetmeats soaked in liquorice and thyme.

The Princess glowed, her skin appeared transparent.
They marvelled at her manners as she whispered
to herself, I have quelled and quelled again
the nature of the toad. A silence fell -
it was her turn to speak. She rose but saw
before her, close at hand, a clan of flies
rejoicing in the vapours of the meat.
Her tongue, prepared for speech, instead flicked out,
and wiped the insects from the startled air.

The star-singer - he who tutored her in magick -
saw her looking pale and green, unearthly,
beside the drooping lilies of her pond,
and in the moment of the moon in the arc
of the swamp, he said, it was a dream
a poor translation, nothing more.

THE POEM OF THE SELF

It is not like any thing.
Not like a window with a blind
through which the Godhead tries to shine.
Not like a candle
consumed by darkness.
Not like a word of music in a song.
Not like the symbols of the heart, the cold and warm.

Not like air, not like water, not like earth, not like fire.

Not like likeness, nor unlikeness.
Not like the living or the dead.
Not like the plant, the animal or the stone.

Here the free word, like unto itself:
I.

DEATH OF A LEAF

The leaf is dead.
The spaces show between its veins -
capillaries cracked where caterpillars used to eat.
Its skeleton is pushing out.

Then, at the gate of death,
all acid leaked out into grass,
do I explain my fear by reference to leaves?

IN THE AIRPORT CONCOURSE

The lighting here shall importune
flesh to become plastic,
that all lit things must seem
so deeply unillumined.
Like gamma rays from outer space this fluorescence turns
once ordinary people into strangers:
dull men of the black or blue or grey suit,
a cult of aliens.

All who are so changed
grow waxen, fleshless, crumpled by degrees,
and sport a paunch. If any one of them
could then bring back the child he had been,
to watch, it would not know,
with its frightened eyes,
what terrible wrath had made it so.

I FAVOUR

I favour the heat from the trees
    to be my fire in winter,
I favour the light from your body, your mind
    flaming, with some parts ashed and crumbling,

I favour what you don't know
    to be the silence I am settling for,
and what I don't know
    to be its other hand:

Come, with one cymbal, never speak to me lies,
    let the cold be our standard,
the flame in the quarrelsome darkness
    quelling black ash.

Ranald Macdonald

George Garson

THE CRUEL MONTH

Closing the door on some TV soap,
we stand in the frozen yard,
hemmed in by stars;
breath crystalline in the night air.
I, filled with daft back-to-nature notions.
He, dragging on a fag: grown gaunt
whilst his yowes fatten on the distant moor.

'There'll be snaw the nicht,' he says,
bunnet peak jabbing Orion below the belt.
I laugh, dismiss his fears as nothing more
than an old hird's tale.
In the morning I awake
to a room scrubbed with light.

A SONG FOR SPRING

I like it fine
when May unwinds and valleys
chime with dollops of cuckoo-call.
I'll hum an artless tune,
test my bones
for time's insiduous betrayal, my lungs,
with a loud hosanna:
close my mind
to winter's carnage of skulls,
and dunk my head in sweet Medwin Water.
Snatch at, and almost grasp,
a split-second
of perpetuity.

DEATH'S REHEARSAL

(Fernihaugh Burial Cairn, October 1989)

When first light stalks across the sheets
and I surface through fragmented dreams,
strictly aligned
like an alabaster donor in a mediaeval nave;
fear-filled, I'll turn onto my side and
slip into a foetal sleep.

Cuddle my lover, death, at the back.
Beaten gold at my throat.
Head crowned with leaves.
Chevroned pots at my feet,
filled with honey and seeds.

MARCH LAMB

She gave birth to her lamb that morning;
a tiny yes
on a frigid hillside.
Twelve ridiculous inches of dazed stuff
sealed in a steaming envelope.

Rising drunkenly on stick-like legs she
ignores her charge,
scarts the frozen ground for heather shoots,
and dreams of dafter days
when scented slopes were randy with tups.

From the edge of the wood,
the dog fox sniffs the infertile air;
smells infant blood.

DEAD YOWE

One would think she had never moved,
my skeletal landmark.
Bones burnished by a presbytery of rooks,
legs abandoned to a celestial jig,
hips at a raunchy angle.

Yet live she surely did.
Clasped dutifully the ram's horny tip;
mithered a wheen o' bairns;
tholed many a winter's grip and
frazzled summers beneath polished skies.

In time, her gaunt posturing will weaken:
become a flattened abstraction,
sundered bits-and-bobs.
A seasoned and sanitised mandible
on a matt-varnished shelf.

George Garson

REVIEWS

OF AFFIRMATION AND THE ABSURD

Coming Down to Earth and Spring is Soon, Robin Fulton, Oasis Books, Shearsman Books; *Salutations: Collected Poems 1960-89*, Alan Jackson, Polygon; *Collected Poems 1958-1982*, George Macbeth, Century Hutchison Ltd, £10.95.

Despite the slightly zany title, *Coming Down to Earth and Spring is Soon*, the tone of these poems is elegiac, as Fulton mourns his pastor father in a style spare as his northern landscape, its "Un-English rocks and rain" - "There are no trees/ north of the north hill." yet even here a "gentle parachute", a tiny seed "aims/ to touch down beside me . . .." Hints of resurrection counterpoint the elegiac tone with "hidden music" and the command (as clearly as in Jackson's *Salutations*) is *'Exultavit'*.

This is a poetry of affirmation: "Some of us/ are still pointing up" declare the old towers of the Hansa town, Lübeck. "Daffodils/ and lit yellow candles" are seen as "giving light/ where nature says there is none." ('Easter Sunday Windows'), and this is not because the dead do not matter, but because they matter too much: "their shadows brighten, not/ darken, everything they touch." ('Requiem'), and "It's/ by their absence the dead give/ countless presence to our steps" ('Multitudes').

Trees, towers, a train journey, the North Sea which separates the poet's homes in Norway and Scotland, a dismantled swing bridge, memories of a walk with his father over old railway tracks, music, a pair of spectacles on the altar of an all-but-redundant Danish church, the Jewish cemetery in Prague all point up the theme. MacDiarmid's "raised beach" is explicit in these poems, but where MacDiarmid finds geology indifferent to human need, Robin Fulton finds "minutes that outlast stones"; and "more generous than immortal stones" the poet's dead father gives "back our silences many-fold" to a son who so clearly knows how to listen, and who finds, as the title poems states, a "sense of scale" which "is certain and/ well".

Alan Jackson, too, has won through to his "sense of scale". 'This is I' proclaims this poet of the absurd, the impossible, of celebration, star shine and simple love: "This story/ This dream/ Is all/ I" Having found himself, Jackson can afford to laugh. There are fun poems, like 'Hitch Haiku':

nae hat
and the cauld rain fallin
dearie me

There are moments of celebration like 'Drama':

Fish are coupling
In my soul
Male and Female
Make one whole

How I wish
I was there,
Underwater wedding
Of the dark and fair.

For Jackson wrong is "to involve/ in what's corrupt./ Wrong to use others/ To heal your cut." And the solution:

Don't pretend;
Make no claim
Strip to the bone
And grow again.

Salutations is a poetry of growth. His wit and zany humour have won Alan Jackson friends beyond the narrow circle of poetry readers. His is a poetry which is carefully planned for the page, but demands an audience. Many of these poems simply have to be heard and as, at last, poetry goes beyond the printed page into the pub, the market place, the meeting place, *Salutations* will find an audience which will welcome its accessibility, buy it, and still find much to ponder on the printed page.

Like Robin Fulton, Alan Jackson has learnt to listen. He has heard the lies which pass for civilisation but which create defences between people and divisions within the self, and having reached a place where he could ask "let me be useless . . ." this poet found the freedom to live. Willing to survive "just ahead of hunger" Jackson joins the joyous "company of dolphins . . . on a voyage of discovery". Polygon is to be congratulated on allowing readers to join this poet's journey to "the heart of the sun" where

The golden grains of love
Lie scattered on the floor
Where does the trail begin?
My friend, at your door.

George Macbeth's *Collected Poems* cover almost quarter of a century. Like Fulton, he mourns his lost father who died during the war "in fire/ Charred in a Sheffield blitz". The poet's dead parents feature in a number of poems, glimpses of their lives recreated through their belongings, a crocodile handbag, a draughtsman's compasses, a miner's helmet:

My father wore it working coal at Shotts
When I was one. My mother stirred his broth
And rocked my cradle with her shivering hands
While this black helemet's long-lost
                              miner's lamp
Showed him the road home.
                    ('The Miner's Helmet')

George Macbeth is skilled in his use of metre and form. There are rhyme schemes, worked to the point of virtuosity: for example the sixteen stanzas of 'An Elegy' are linked by the caesura which runs in every case from the last line of the previous stanza, the rhyme scheme throughout being abcbac. "The Crab-Apple Crisis is worked out on the levels and rungs of Herman Kahn's "metaphysical ladder" showing the paths "between a low-level crisis and an all-out war." 'Fin du Globe' is formatted like a game "with a dealer and four players". 'What Meter Is' demonstrates various possiblities - "Internal/ rhyming . . . is/ a matter of timing," taking us through 'At the House of Jade', 'Pavan for an Unborn Infanta', 'The Lax Cheer' which are set out in columns and groups of syllables - clever stuff, doubtless, but it leaves me cold. Similarly, lines like "Her breasts/ under her wool sweater/ heave and invite . . ." and, "For Christ's sake take me home/ and screw me, man" might have been trendy in the swinging sixties but jar as poetry. Totally distasteful to me is 'The Auschwitz Rag'. I much prefer the mellow tone of what seem to me mature and genuine poems with which the collection ends, when the poet has loved and lost, fathered children and reached a point of hope and affirmation. "I've come of age . . . I'll be an acolyte of vivid hue,/ And let the dead/ Lie dim and simple in their cold./ A time for grins/ is come, for jousting crimson, all things new."

Jenny Robertson

TENNIS WITH, AND WITHOUT, A NET

Madam Doubtfire's Dilemma, Dilys Rose, Chapman £4.50; *Varying States of Grace*, Ian Stephen, Polygon £6.95; *Darkness and Snowfall*, Andrew Fox, Blind Serpent Press £3.90; *Technologies and Other Poems*, Gerrie Fellows, Polygon £6.95

I like Dilys Rose's book for its clarity, depiction of characters and situations, its lack of fake obscurantism, its non-pompous *entertainment*. A woman's view of the world, not without an ironic look at the bumbling male in the "drunken men folk on the terrace", the tattoo done "last night: behind the blinds of Alf's Art Parlour" and the philandering lecturer who "wears a wide-brimmed hat these days/ to shade his eyes and cover what's left/ of his hair." She pokes tragi-comic fun at her own sex too in 'Succubus': "I remember when any old plonk/ Would do, but let that pass . . . The talk? I whisked it away/ from the indigestible." And more seriously the controlled emotion of 'A Beginning', which portrays the sick husband of an apparently indifferent marriage and his widow's self-reliance. Two characters in sixteen lines and the seeds of what is often,

nowadays, the whole matter of a novel.

I liked 'The World About Us' where the life of plants is contrasted approvingly with other biological forms. Less approving and more allegorical is 'Queen Bee' who "squeezed what she could/ from her loyal industrious crew" and ends by "Drunkenly weeping/ Bittersweet regal tears." The grim facts of our all-eat-all condition are depicted in fleshly detail in a poem about shelling scallops: "I gouge out the edible bite/ Chuck the guts overboard" contrasts with the beauty of the shells' fanlike pattern. Rose's poetry has intelligence and a real humanity the reader can share, a pleasurable antidote after the usual chore of wading through cryptograms to find that, in the end, gassy borborygms are all that remain. But this collection is no simple-Simon poetry, but informed by a sharp wit and a learned mind.

Ian Stephen is a coastguard on Lewis. Much of the work is experience recollected, if not in tranquillity, then in distance from the subject. 'Shotts 1985' - "bleary pitheads where sleet hangs about the bings" - is a long way from the high-sounding surf of the Hebrides in more ways than geography. Stephen cuts the cackle and comes to the horses; remembering Jeannie Robertson's singing he says: "the husk, the grain-rough/ soreness in the throat . . . not a caramel trace in what she gave . . ." and a Hamish Henderson recital evokes: "this was recorded in Carrara . . ./ and I heard the cleft sparks; tasted marble dust in my nostrils". Talking of a Gaelic poet (Sorley MacLean?) reciting in Edinburgh he asks "what makes lines strong/ an adolescence of energy/ in a stormy co-existence/ . . . with hours of skill."

Although Stephen's poetry draws inspiration from Zurich, Hamburg, Reykjavik, Bayonne, his standing place is Scotland. The hallmarks are there in the contemplations of religion both local: "Church, for me, was *The Water Babies/* . . .taken to our pew with Dolly Mixtures which didn't crunch" and later in a Basque church; in the sense of origins both geographic and genealogical, in the taste for stark landscape as in 'Scapa Shore' where the eye is taken by "a blackened spine and oak ribs . . . boat's remains". Landscape (and indeed city-scape) are the source of much of the verse. In 'They Kill Sheep' rural necessity is drawn without sentiment, but I bet that if this poem had been written in Scots some ignorant ass would describe it as "kailyard", which it certainly is not. A neat book, easily carried in the pocket.

There is something Larkin-like in Andrew Fox's 'Memories of Eden', but instead of the incongruous bicycle clips in an empty church we have pebbled lenses steaming up in a noisy swimming bath. In 'Dentist' he sits apprehensively as the tooth-expert "hooks the nozzle/ of an air-jet over my lower lip/ . . . as if I were a giant fish hauled up from the depths." These give one the impression of a person without help in the face of circumstance: our common fate, vividly depicted. Once more, praise be, the poet is concerned with countryside, landscape. Andrew Fox likes swans, terns, cumulus, ploughed fields, meadows, reeds and the *hiraeth* of old legend. Helen, Leda, warrior princes become again the theme of a poem. There is regard for the one unmentionable thing of our frank and open times: mortality. 'For Hugo Barber, Drowned' and become "one of the numberless waves stunned/ and broken by the shore". Different, but no less dead, 'Commando' "lies prone on the rippling sand/ in the open grave of the desert". There are poems about painters: Rousseau, Rembrandt. From the Douanier " . . a spark of lightning darts along/ his brush and he sees/ a tiger", while the Dutchman contemplates "the harmonies that join the living to the dead."

Gerrie Fellows trained as a painter and spent time in art schools, so it is not surprising that she, too, should write poems about landscape, terrain, pictures, constructions. Not that this book is really about painting as such; but there is a strong feeling for the visual impact of natural features, street scenes, journeys. The title poem has the theme of Eskimo life. "Carved hooks are cut for use/ . . . dogwhip thimble ivory /snowknife". 'The Unrecorded' is about the Armenian earthquake disaster. "In the dark . . . small voices cry . . . the mouths of the survivors . . . are black holes."

The poems of Dilys Rose and Stephen pay some respect to poetic form in the matter of rhythm. Those of Fox and Gerrie Fellows are looser. I suppose the lines are split where the poets perceive a caesura, but to my ear some of these breaks seem totally arbitrary, the displacement of words and phrases merely precious. Fellows also leaves spaces of varying length between words, presumably to indicate the length of pauses. This is a matter of taste. But if writing free verse is like playing tennis without a net, removal of the white lines and the umpire spoils the whole game and makes everyone a champion. The best 20th century poets could all write fine, flowing stanzas. 'J. Alfred Prufrock', that most modern of poems, was written in verse which had form, by a poet who knew about prosody. Prose may be poetic, but all that is not verse is prose. The demanding forms of Wyatt and Yeats are unfashionable, but a look back through poetic history requires that 'modern' poets learn that form enhances art. Free verse is fine in reasonable doses. Unremitting free verse is every bit as monotonous as tum-ti-tum rhythm. If you've no eye for composition, don't paint. If you simply *can't* write the odd formal stanza, stick to prose.   - William Neill

A POETIC SESTET

The Scampering Marmoset, Ken Morrice, Aberdeen UP; *Waiting for the Storm*, Gerald Mangan, Bloodaxe £5.95); *Rock and Water*, Aonghas MacNeacail, Polygon £6.95; *Advice to Travellers*, Stanley Roger Green, AUP £6.95; *Selected Poems 1970-1990*, Donald Campbell, £4.95; *The Moon Calf*, Alexander Hutchinson, both Galliard £6.95

None of these poets is in the first flush of youth (more than one refers to the ageing process). But each has quite a time yet before he becomes a Scottish literary grandee. For that distinction, you have to be male of course (they all qualify on that score), and preferably septuagenarian.

Ken Morrice brings to his poetry a scientific background. Being a psychiatrist, it puts him in an unusual position *vis-a-vis* his creativity. So often the artist or poet identifies with the powerless. Morrice, however, is by profession one of the powerful but has the character to see beyond his position, understanding the powerless. In 'Occupational Therapy', he gives a compassionate but telling overview of the way the damaged psyche is tackled professionally - "So activity fills love's lack," Patients are cajoled into basket-making, a ploy that is a poor substitute for their *real* needs.

Sometimes Morrice seems an elegant nihilist, resigned to lead an uneventful existence in a decorous sort of way. He can encapsulate the 'here and now' (which he never shirks) aptly - even beautifully. And he has a heart; his poetry never bamboozles with technique or obscurity - he's too interested in conveying his message.

It's easy to like this man. His birthday poem for his wife: "I am content with what I have in life" other tributes to women close to him - his daughter and mother - all suggest an open, clear, honest chap. Take 'Snob', where he admits he's too upmarket for most of the punters who go to football matches: "But the Proletariat/ are not starey-at,/ I just don't enjoy/ hoi-polloi." I don't always find his language arresting. It's homely enough, but not very stylish, with some adjectives and imagery a little too expected. 'Alien' is about a visit to India and his encounter with a holy man, but it seems flabby: "I walk past girls in pretty saris,/ dark shops bright with mangoes,/ coconuts, pineapples, and plantains."

My favourite poems in this, Morrice's sixth collection, are those that hark back to the past, which he compares to our present bereft times. 'Old Torry' explains wistfully how the fishing industry has been taken over by the oil boom. In 'Defector', Morrice asks if today we experience a better quality of life than yesterday: "I have forsaken/ your toil, your Kirk, the old ways/ of poverty and submission." This poem is a lyrical

cry of great yearning and tremendous regret:

I long for old familiar faces,
remembering warm loving childhood places,
slow speech and walk - safer, kindlier
times than this!

For years, Gerald Mangan has been publishing poems in literary magazines. *Waiting for the Storm* is his long-awaited first collection. His is a careful hand - not too spare or condensed, or prolix. Mangan achieves a nice tension that isn't staccato or jerky, and his metaphors can be tight. His imagery is neither startlingly outlandish nor too predictable. He is a poet who evidently has deep feelings, his themes exile, decay and destruction (among others). But his commitment never obtrudes his work's form and grace.

The poet's Glasgow poems are particularly interesting, partly because, unlike Tom Leonard or Liz Lochhead, Mangan is removed from the city. He doesn't espouse it, but looks at it from afar - as an exile. The issue is treated simply in 'Death of an Islandman' where, listening to music in a Glasgow flat, an old man remembers his earlier island life. It's a masterful picture, drawn economically in six verses of four short lines:

Docked in a high tenement,
where the light-bulb hangs by a hair
he listens to the cistern fill,
and hears the tide at the harbour wall.

Destruction is expressed in 'New City Road', executed in an old-fashioned metre with a refrain of couplets. The neat, excellently-chosen quotation at the head of the poem by Baudelaire, gives an added dimension - "The shape of a town changes faster, sadly, than the human heart." Mangan enjoys parody, even pastiche, and most memorable in this genre is his excoriating 'Scotland the Ghost'. Here, the poet paints this country as a body - or an animated corpse - whose career he outlines from Wallace to Queen Victoria: "It drags the sword of Wallace, it's lugging Bruce's helmet;/ But spiders make their webs in it, and a draught would overwhelm it./ The heart inside the armour's like the queen inside her cell:/ The breath of Knox has chilled it, and blasted it to hell." This poem does a marvellous purge on all Lauderism or Caledonian kitsch.

For pure pastiche, there's also Mangan's 'Laird of Ardluggan', biting in its satire, but terribly true with a portrait that shows the man as "all Gordonstoun plums, and Balliol pebbles." I love his terse observation of England in 'The Midland Scot': "A country for counting/ potting-sheds like sheep." 'Edinburgh' is a summing up in toto of the quintessential nature of the capital, by the use of a portrait of a landlady. This poet is excellent in finding the right word for the correct image:

She learnt her poise with a book on her head,
but it's capital that keeps it high.
Her bank's no castle in the air,
but a church grounded in rock.

He is best at catching evanescence, booking the fleeting moment, as in 'Leaving Dieppe':

I hold on hard, at the stern-rail,
to that last wave you gave:
the way it fell, as the guard whistled,
and you pressed a kiss to the glass.

Few poets can now write about a community that's intact. More often, their subject today is of dislocation, even dismemberment. But, in *Rock and Water*, the Skye-born poet Aonghas MacNeacail presents a society that, although (some might argue) severely dented - even rent apart at the roots - still contains relics of cohesion.

Rock and Water reveals a variety of characters, from sailors to ministers and tinkers, people of an implicit order, thoroughly known amongst each other, of an implicit order. In fact, the impression accrued of blaeberry picking, Sunday schools, following the dung cart, and stalwart individuals like Murdo Mackenzie, the Piper, remind me of the community in Dylan Thomas's *Under Milk Wood*. MacNeacail can draw lovely portraits: Ma Macrimmon standing by the roadside waiting for her son, Jimmy, to come home from the sea, hopelessly drunk. Here the poet is acting as the bard, recording people's lives.

MacNeacail writes in English, his second language, achieving a fluidity in his unusual structures. It's soft and undulating in rhythm - like the incessant movement of waves, of crescendo and diminuendo, and no jarring stops, eschewing full-stops and employing only lower-case characters. It all adds up to a sense of modernity - old themes being told in a new way. Several polemical prose pieces interrupt the poetry. One is on anglicisation in Skye. Most telling is the story of a factor who lost his mind because no-one on the island would speak to him in English "as if this ignoring of him would cut the wound even deeper." MacNeacail's valedictory prose piece expresses his feeling that as writer/poet, he *must* be involved with the destiny of his own race. *His* way is to listen to what his people sing (therein one finds the truth) and put it into his poetry.

The poet is fresh and melodious in approach, but never lets reality or history off the hook. Not far below the surface is anger at what's happened to the Gael. In 'Country Life', a crofter labours at working his sour land: "GOD DAMN this earth, when not alive/ with stone, it's bog, and always greedy/ for dung." In 'Law and Order', it's the Laird who is the *real* thief, and the islander never locks his door except when tourists come.

MacNeacail is best, however, when he makes statements obliquely, as in 'Dispatches', which is concerned with emigration. He describes Archie, the postman, bringing letters to the islanders from relatives as far-flung as New Zealand, Glasgow and Cape Breton. Less allusive and more direct is 'Prime of Life': "the young have left/ a place propped up on the frail/ bones of pensioners./ crofts die under docken thistles nettles and/ the absence of livestock." The poet can switch from pain, loss, anger and regret to a tender, loving mood. His love poetry is delightful. 'Beyond the Diamond' expresses well-seasoned love perfectly: "They do not touch except in turning over/during sleep."

Stanley Roger Green's *Advice to Travellers* is uneven. In places, I find him wordy, his imagery flaccid and old-fashioned, as in 'Albatross': "Day after doldrum day aloft", and in 'Bay Horses': "Like a flight of plumed arrows winging/ Above glinting snow and frozen streams." In other places, his verse can be inaccessible and unbending, with little elasticity to the rhythm.

Many are about places Green has travelled: Bermuda, Tripoli, Rhodes and other Islands in the Aegean. He writes of these areas as a bystander with no real gut feeling for what he observes - which makes the work peculiarly unanimated. Green improves when he becomes involved with his subject. 'My Father' is interesting, though he tries too hard with the odd purple phrase: "The ice-veined widow-maker/ Gathering him in wintry folds:"

I go for his poems on flora, fauna and nature in general; in these, he uses a miniaturist's brush to describe a ladybird's movements in 'Threnody':

In emblazoned arrogance that yet delights
When you walk all over me, to become
A sleeve-cuff button, a ruby tie-pin,
A cryptic dominoed badge on my lapel;

In 'He bought her red roses', the poet strikes a crisp, balanced note on rejection. And 'Skating on Dunsapie' (remember Raeburn's painting of the solemn minister on ice) represents his philosophic and ruminative proclivities:

Bottomless too is the outstretched mind;
But we only strive to reach the other side
And hope the thin ice will not break.

He can be devastatingly truthful and even unpleasant in his accuracy in 'Nostalgic Encounter' where he describes a meeting with an old flame that has obviously diminished to only a flicker. His sensuous evocation of nature delights me in 'The Heart of the Hills': "I see glowing under a bracken spray/ The year's first ripened blaeberry,/ Secret, globular and· dusky blue -".

The series of poems on birds, the lark, swallow and starling, have a verve and an impression of space, lacking in the others. In 'Lark Singing', Green's sensitive treatment reveals the energy within. He can be cleverly onomatopoeic in choosing words that suggest the cheeky starling:

the townie birds,
Riff-raff of dawn choristers,
Suddenly lunging from one bush
To another for no reason at all.

The rendering of a scene in the Summer Isles deserves a mention finally, where Green lovingly tells of the antics of the seals: "And roll slug-like from slimed rocks/ to belly-flop into ringmasters/ Of their own sleek circuses". Stanley Roger Green should let himself go in his poetry; he has the technique and the magnanimity. Only, I think he's afraid of applying the latter.

The same cannot be said of Donald Campbell. He applies plenty of both: lots of technique and plenty of guts and heart. Here is a poet, as MacDiarmid is purported to have claimed, who is "alive in his own time".

Campbell has an astonishing ear, musicality and assurance. His work is written to be heard rather than read, and he writes mainly in Scots - Edinburgh Scots. His fresh dynamism doesn't trip you up as it might in denser, less talented writers. Since it is my second language, I generally find Scots hard to understand: not with Campbell, though. As expected with a musical poet, his poetry enjoys refrains, repetitions and questions, and can seem quite traditional, but I think this traditionalism is dictated by the language. Unlike English (or English translations of Gaelic) Scots commands its own particular form and rhythm.

Campbell examines the languages Scots and English in 'Bilingual Manifesto' and in 'Ye Say "Glass"'; the former crystallising the Scottish dilemma or Caledonian antizysygy. "Whyles I try to write in English/ Sometimes/ I ettle to scrieve in Scots." The latter reminds me of MacDiarmid's short poem about the word 'British', and how it is anathema to him because with one letter it can be changed to 'Brutish'. Campbell makes the point similarly with 'glass', and how by changing the vowel, it has a different timbre - 'gless'.

Although he can be serious, Campbell is also an entertainer, light-hearted and funny as in 'See You!', where he lists a number of denigrating appellations alliteratively to his subject, showing that Scots can be so much more descriptive than English: "See you?/ ye gaighie/ ye dummeral/ ye gowkish, glaikit gommeral."

Campbell and urban, up-to-the-minute Edinburgh (not the New Town, but more the Old before it was mummified by museums and gentrified out of recognition) is reminiscent of Tom

Leonard and Glasgow. A comprehensive panoramic view of the capital is offered; 'Betrayal in Morningside' explains how Edinburgh is lumbered with a deadlier breed of hard man than Glasgow. The tenement block and "the perennial stair" features as does 'Daft Jock', the tramp who wants to read in the public library.

Being a playwright, Campbell, in this collection spanning twenty-odd years, includes songs from his shows, like 'Blackfriar's Wynd'. 'Vietnam on My Mind' reminds me of the comment by Ralph Waldo Emerson, "your goodness abroad is spite at home". The man in this poem overlooks his wife being raped and a boy falling out of a window because he's too preoccupied with brooding over Vietnam. It proves that when philosophising or making a serious point, Scots isn't as dry or laboured as the equivalent in English.

The final section - a respectful tribute to women - reads well. In Scots, there is a danger that in attempting to be tender the poet can lapse into sentimentality. These poems are thoughtful, even profound, like the ones to the Caithness granny and to Joan Ure. In 'Woman Washing', Campbell notices with precision how a woman's strength differs from a man's: "Female/ muscle is made/ for the lang tyauve, the sair trail./ No sudden, but shair./ Never strang, but aye siccar."

Alexander Hutchinson's The Moon Calf is a varied collection. Hutchinson likes word-play, the abbreviated and the staccato. His poetry is anglicised or transatlanticised (Hutchinson spent almost twenty years in Canada teaching literature and writing at the University of Victoria). Some of his work gives the impression of being carefully written, rather academic - representative of the post-modernist movement, with its cool (sometimes almost soulless) rhythms. In 'Je Brule comme une cloche' as with other examples, he plays with space on the page - accommodating solely two or three words to a line. The effect of this is of undulation and of an unceasing movement - pleasant and modern in effect.

Hutchinson's ability to tell the painful truth is shown in 'The Usual Story', a marvellous poem on the post mortem of a love affair or marriage: "he became a block of ice/ she ran to seed/ he became a block of stone/ she started chipping/ he dreamed his best dream/ she sealed him in". Largely, I prefer his translations and the final poem, 'Inchcolm'. It's a spot of genius for him to take a poet like Catullus and translate him into Scots. Being raunchy and salacious, the earthy Roman lends himself to Scots more than English, which never manages to sound right when describing such sentiments. Hutchinson, who often writes Scots phonetically, achieves a colloqial, chatty tenor in these eight poems:

Yer very cack-hold rins clear
as a cellar a saat. Ye quidna shite
nor ten times a twal-month.
An syne it's as hard as a bool
a bean. Roll't or rub't in
yer haun - it widna even blaud
yer finger-end.

Salty, smutty, basic stuff, but direct, and congratulations to Galliard for including a glossary.

Part of Hutchinson's contribution in Scots is a translation of four poems by the 16th century French poet Pierre de Ronsard. I assume that this distance of time, an age so different to our own, helps him to write his translations in Scots. Or is he trying to evade the problem that some poets have with Scots, of not finding it contemporary or modern enough when used to express serious issues? No matter. Ronsard brings a note of elegance and seriousness to these love sonnets.

If a certain lack of juice can be detected in Hutchinson, then the sap is reinstated in 'Inchcolm', which is unquirky and straightforward, coming directly from the heart: 'Whatever evil the tongue composes/ conscience may overcome.' With its tranquil, reverberating echoes, he travels with composure through the centuries. It needs no explanation, only quotation:

Within this high-vaulted
chamber I show you to shadows: the dreaming
forms of those who sleep like mist, who looked
in their own way for what holds true beneath
the bewilderment of surfaces.

Mary Gladstone

NOVELS OF INTOLERATION

Ballad of Sawney Bain, Harry Tait, Polygon, £9.95; The Pale Criminal, Philip Kerr, Viking, £13.99

Harry Tait's first novel The Ballad of Sawney Bain, a gigantic study of Covenanting times in the 17th century, is a remarkable piece of work. It is the saga of Sawney, a soldier of fortune, his wife Black Agnes Douglas, and their friend Steenie Malecky. When Sawney and Steenie return from the wars in Germany, fighting with General Leslie's army for King Gustaphus Adolphus, they settle in their native Galloway, where Sawney and Agnes, whom he had sworn when she was a child to marry, take up residence in a cave on the Solway Firth. But they are not allowed to live in peace. Two ministers of the kirk, Willie Munro and Mathius Pringle, persecute them in wildly imaginative, bigoted sermons. Sawney is branded as a cannibal, Black Agnes and her mother Janet are heralded as witches, and Steenie, of whose intellect and erudition the ministers are madly jealous, is labelled a warlock.

This persecution lasts for years. Sawney goes back to fighting on the continent. Agnes and Steenie travel to the Highlands to escape the invective of the ministers and the trouble it causes among the Covenanters. They run into Montrose and his army fighting for the King, and have an uneasy relationship with the great Marquis. After Montrose's sack of the city of Aberdeen, they flee to the comparative safety of the clan known as the People of the Mist (the outlawed MacGregors) and Agnes has a lesbian affair with Catriona, the chief's daughter, who has the second sight.

The plot is too complicated to summarise clearly, but it is enough to say that it is a vigorous tale, full of surprises and macabre and evil happenings. In the long run they all become victims of the bigotry and cruelty of the Covenanters. The book starts with Sawney, as an old man, after he'd been tortured, being interviewed by the monster of a minister.

The Covenanters were tremendous bigots, and this bigotry lingers on in the Scottish kirk to this day. The utterly religious Scot is a menace, intolerant of all other outlooks and creeds. Unfortunately, Mr Tait repeats the same kind of sermonising so often that it becomes wearisome and loses impact. I was forced to skip long passages, passages that would have been more effective if they had been editorially pruned. My hand itched, and I kept wishing I was still a publisher's editor and could cut it as I cut so many longwinded books in years gone by.

The fact that the narrative is partly written in broad Scots and partly in pulpit English also makes it a difficult read. Nevertheless, it is a clever unveiling of Covenanting cruelty, bigotry and intolerance. Sawney Bain has won the Saltire Literary Award for the Scottish First Book of the Year. It truly deserves to be the winner.

The Pale Criminal is another novel about intolerance, this time of the Nazis for the Jews. Private detective Bernie Gunther, who has already appeared in Philip Kerr's first novel March Violets (Penguin Books £3.99) investigates a series of bizarre murders of young girls, all Jews, in Berlin in the summer of 1938. Some of the chief Nazi leaders appear in the story, including Himmler, who attends a bogus seance. Bernie begins to suspect that Julius Streicher, editor of the Jew-baiting paper Der Sturmer, whose favourite pastime is whipping young boys, is the murderer. It's a little far-fetched, and Philip Kerr's characters seem to belong more to the 1980s than the 1930s. However, it is entertaining, though I read it with the same feeling of disbelief that I have when watching a James Bond film.

Fred Urquhart

A CACHE OF CRITICS

The Rise of the Historical Novel: The Enlightenment and Scottish Literature Pt II, John MacQueen, Scottish Academic Press, £16.50, Bryght Lanternis, Essays on the Language and Literature of Renaissance Scotland, ed J D McClure/M.R.G. Spiller, AUP £16.50. Studies in Scottish Fiction: Twentieth Century, ed J Schwend/H.W. Drescher, DM93, James Hogg: Poetic Mirrors ed David Groves DM77, Modernism in the Second World War, Keith Alldritt $37.95 (all Peter Lang). Byron and Scotland ed Angus Calder, EUP, £12.

John MacQueen's 1982 Progress and Poetry was an odd masterpiece, deceptively slight-looking. He doesn't go on much about the change in Weltanschauung which distinguishes Burns from Fergusson: but says everything. After a time the force of his judgments strike the re-reader quite hard: one should worry about disagreeing with him; and even where disagreement persists, MacQueen retains a huge capacity to inform. There is nothing impressionistic, also no getting lost in the very intensive detail. Its Prolegomenon is one of the most generally informative writings of all on the Scottish 18th century. Indeed he has something fresh and maybe definitive to say about the debatable term 'Scottish Enlightenment' itself!

He gives an intensive study of Scott's practice, his use of Shakespearean and Sophoclean models like George Douglas Brown and James Joyce. The Scott unenthusiast can still be grateful for that non-judgmental exposition: are the "calm passions" of Smith and Hume part of man's eternal frame since the coming of some 'Enlightenment', the psychology of St Ronan's Well applying, rather than the Iliad? There is comparable depth to the book's Epilogue on Carlyle, whose "reaction against the Enlightenment might have increased its intellectual and imaginative effect, had his eyes been more opened . . . to the distinctively Scottish experience of the centuries". Carlyle cites German examples - not Henryson. But by the end of the third chapter, on Galt, the case is presented of an author so involved in both Scottish-historical detail and supposed laws of Scottish-historical development, as almost to have lost sight of universals, specialist fashion. Did the "strange death of Scottish history" occur from an excess of it? There is something oppressive in the Galt MacQueen delineates, obsessed with Scottish history and a specialised untranslatable version of it.

It is a relief to find the excellent, even longer chapter on James Hogg, who happily has nothing to do with either the Enlightenment or the Historical Novel; and is a vastly superior moral psychologist for all that! While much could be argued beyond this book, its substance renders it absolutely necessary reading in the field: a huge contribution to wider debates, expository work such as one is seldom privileged to read.

Bryght Lanternis is part of another important movement in which John MacQueen has a big part. Understanding of 'Mediaeval and Renaissance Scotland' is not yet as it ought to be, and Rod Lyall's essay here shows how much has been lost of a large and distinguished literature: what matters is not the sort of theory insisting on (to Lyall's justifiable disdain) the alterity/essential otherness of mediaeval literature. Rather we need the careful historical work to reveal the depth of culture of a period which includes Robert Carver (1487-1566) the composer (here well discussed by Richard Turbet), the John Knox nobody knows, The Book of the Dean of Lismore. Fionn MacColla went too far, saying the Reformation strangled at birth the greatest cultural flowering in the history of Europe. But how far from parochial was pre-1603 Scottish culture. With abstruse discussions of language and fascinating essays on Dunbar, the folk background, the philosopher John Ireland et al., this is a delightful evocation of decently scholarly culture.

And Schwend & Drescher's miscellany on 20th century Scottish fiction? One danger of taking modern Scottish novels too seriously is of letting standards plummet: another is infection from today's publish-or-perish desperation. There is a panel which awards tin badges for what members of staff of UK university depts. publish in his/her field. Win no badges, you risk your dept/faculty- (!!!) getting the chop like Strathclyde University Philosophy section! With no consideration of the quality or worth of what appears! Alas while Schwend's essay on the Kirk in 20th century Scottish fiction is above suspicion of badge-hunting, it explores a theme without reference to the literary interest of the works in which it appears. To what extent can any treatment be counted if a product of publishing opportunism or a casual jeu d'esprit? Elsewhere obsessive rot about Edwin Muir, bad literary theory mechanically applied, overbiographical comment on Naomi Mitchison, an essay on Neil Gunn subtitled 'The Anxiety of Influence' after a sterile coinage by the rather fanciful Harold Bloom. Caution is advised. Willa Muir, George Blake, Nan Shepherd, Lorna Moon, David Lindsay, Buchan, George Douglas Brown's not so marginal alia; Gibbon, Mackenzie, city novel: a mixture of the acute and the appalling to be found in Scot Lit Depts today, on a wide range of modern Scottish fiction.

Easier reading is the Byron, but its conclusion by Drummond Bone is more an act of faith in the categories of his own academic category than a bringing together of the book's very various material: Galt & Byron, Byron & Scott, interestingly Byron and (Roman) Catholicism, &c., at various levels from the literate popular. Too much a mixture to come off easily, is its being the book of the conference a good thing: contributors gathered on a 'who'llwehaveattheparty' basis, the flavour more of a periodical than the hardback book? It isn't nostalgia makes one relish the late Norman Buchan's Preface, conjuring visions of what Byron's muse would sing confronted by Mgt. Thtchr's 'Sermon on the Mound' and contrasting our present day liberty (under a Triumdiabolate of Press Barons) with the complex of liberty/suppression of Byron's time. A major omission is surely of reference to Byron's influence on Russia: "Niet, ne Byron . . . ", wrote Lermontov, very significantly.

Keith Alldritt is a good critic, his book here a sad botch. Its survey of W.W. II poetry suggests unfortunately scant knowledge beyond say Alun Lewis, and little about the 'Apocalyptics', who are sidelined with an inept phrase. The potted biography of MacDiarmid cuts all the wrong corners and is wrong. The idea is good: discuss substantial wartime work by Eliot, Pound, Bunting, MacDiarmid. There is acute comment amid collapse into error (Largo Law, in Bunting's The Spoils is not a harbour but a hill - how else 'look down' from it!) or a kind of padding. Marks deducted for failure of thoroughness, though despite the blunders there are sharp insights.

And then we have James Hogg. The Poetic Mirror is a masterpiece of parody, of Crabbe and other contemporaries of Hogg, in remarkable style: the most difficult not least valuable kind of criticism. One should not think of Hogg without recognising what is implied by the howlingly funny parody of Wordsworth, 'The Flying Tailor': among the most astounding in the English language.

A dismal omen! that to mind like his,
Apt to perceive in slightest circumstance
Mysterious meaning, yielded sore distress
And feverish perturbation, so that oft
He scarce could eat his dinner - . . .

. . . For mark my words, - eternally my name
Shall last on earth, conspicuous like a star
'Mid that bright galaxy of favoured spirits,
Who, laugh'd at constantly whene'er
                        they published,
Survived the impotent scorn of base Reviews,
Monthly or Quarterly, or that accursed
Journal, the Edinburgh Review, that lives
On tears, and sighs, and groans,
                     and brains, and blood.

David Groves's edition is impeccable, with valuable apparatus.   Robert Calder

Kisties

McGinn of the Calton, Greentrax Records; *Rhyme & Reason,* Nancy Nicholson, Gallus Music, 187 Wilton St, Glasgow, £5.99; *Songs from Under the Bed No 2,* Various artists, *To Paint the Green Hill Brown,* Tony MacManus, both Cora-Linn Music, 37 Claremont Bank, Edinburgh; *Clearsong,* Sheena Wellington, Dunkeld Records, Old Schoolhouse, Butterstone, Dunkeld, £6.25; *Nippit Fit Clippit Fit,* Stanley Robertson, Aberdeen City Libraries, Rosemount Viaduct, AB1 1GU, £5.50.

When and if the dust settles on this century it will leave millions of miles of cassette tapes that could provide a bewildering variety of listening. Even within the relatively homogenous species of 'Folk Song' tapes in the above list is such a variety of approach and content as to attract or repel individual tastes. They are all, however, Scottish in origin and all but one commit themselves to politics or political stances.

Greentrax Records' lavishly long celebratory cassette (1 hr 26 mins) in appreciation of the stories and songs of Matt McGinn of the Calton. This energetic and varied tribute is presented through a linked commentary by Adam Mac-Naughtan and the music and songs of Matt McGinn performed by Stramash. This tape offers a signal service by bringing together this aural evocation of the multi-faceted McGinn from the wistfully reflective 'Magic Shadow Show' which, fittingly, tops and tails the cassette, through flights of extravagant daftness as in 'The Red Yo-Yo', tender lullaby ('Coorie Doon'), to sincere love song ('Jeannie Gallagher'), and naked self-scrutiny ('Troubled Waters in my Soul'). McGinn's passionate political commitment is expressed in satiric catchy choruses like 'Three nights and a Sunday double-time', songs of cameraderie like 'The can o' tea', and in visionary incantations ('We'll Have a May-Day'). The individual variety of the members of Stramash in presenting these aspects of McGinn serve his memory and his work with sensitivity, sincerity and accomplishment.

In Nuclear Caithness atoms are good news,
They brought us jobs and money,
we'd be stupid to refuse.
So now we've nuclear fish, fine atomic coos,
Plutonium-plated people and
radioactive booze.

In often deceptively simple rhymes Nancy Nicholson, thirled to her native Caithness, reasons her singing protests at the defilement of that land and its people. Her use of innocent-sounding merry little children's tunes, sung without adornment, sends a chilling frisson through such lightly sung lines from 'Last Carol' as "Mushroom cloud and heavy water/ My last son and your last daughter/ White and sear the blasted ground/ Husha, husha, all fall down." They echo the blandness which characterises official and public acceptance of nuclear hazards and the very simplicity of the lines is their efficacy. Other pet quarries for Nancy's satiric darts of song are those of the Scottish teaching profession, still too astonishingly many, who cripple the spirit of our children by deriding their tongue. In this vein 'Listen to the Teacher' is catchy, mischievous, and hits the mark. The tape is interspersed with Nancy's neat melodeon playing of Scottish airs and dances and concludes, fitting to the warmth and incision of that lady, with her song 'Cuddle against the War': 'Use your arms for cuddling, that's what arms are for.' And so say all of us.

Strange companions gather in *Songs from Under the Bed No 2.* What brings them under the hot-bed is a common commitment to political protest and an impetus for social justice. Protest against injustice, voicing the affront to humanity of violence and prejudice, compassion for the downtrodden, the defeated and the down-and-out have always been themes in the folk-world's attack on complacency and complicity, but to be effective, inspiring or motivating such themes require cogent lyrics, delicate orchestration and subtle management. In areas like this, personal tastes and preferences shape our appreciation, but most of these tracks are relentlessly dunning with a crudity of approach that alienates rather than converts. Exceptional are Hamish Henderson's now thankfully anachronistic 'Free Mandela' which still stands as a rousing piece of song history exemplary in its genre, and his eloquent empathic poem 'The Cell'. But, on the whole, the tape lacks charisma and inclusive humanity. To be *AGAINST* is not enough.

The title *To Paint the Green Hill Brown* comes from lines in Frank O'Connor's translation of the 18th century Irish 'Lament for Yellow-Haired Donough'. The lines are a sad evocation of youth cut down, a generous youth, a beautiful youth held in the image of a young hand behind the plough that no longer will paint the green hill brown. This fresh and resonating image like others in songs on this tape reward hearing again with their sometimes grave, earthy, eerie use of Scots. The setting given to MacDiarmid's mysterious piece from *The Drunk Man Looks at the Thistle,* 'Wha's the bride?' brings out the haunting paradoxical compulsion of that strange, lovely passage. Not all tracks appeal so directly but there is an integrity in Tony McManus's drive to realise his goals that is appealing in this production.

Sheena Wellington's cassette *Clearsong,* produced by Douggie MacLean, conducts you through fluent, well-orchestrated movements of moods. Hers are the politics of the heart so that those songs which deal with the savage in human nature are hued with sadness, a lament for our short-comings: "the thing that we're best at is killing." Kenna Campbell's translation from the Gaelic with Sheena's singing of 'The ChristChild's Lullaby' make a sweet musical marriage and the simple unjudgmental tone in her rendition of Adam MacNaughton's 'Yellow on the Broom' is my favourite version of that song to date. The clarity and quality of the voice reach an absorbing depth of feeling in the final track 'Julia's Song', a benison for a baby in the lovely words, "May you always have rainbows and flowers and song/ May you always have someone to love."

The beguiling feature in story, song or ballad on *Nippit Fit Clippit Fit* is the fulsome North-east rhythm of Stanley Robertson's voice which infuses his presentations in any mode with conviction. This tape is of interest to story-tellers and collectors for its Scottish version of Cinderella, which gives the tape its title, and other such folk tales as that which unfolds the dire fate that befalls the 'wee bannocky' (before it crossed the ocean metamorphosed into 'the gingerbread man'). There are also fun children's pieces like the ditty 'I Chokkit on a Tattie' and Stanley's fine verson of the ballad 'The Laird o' Drum'. This is the only tape without overt political clouts but its final word on the Laird o' Drum has a Dunbar-like sombre egalitarian conclusion:

O when you are dead and I am dead
And in the grave we're laid o
When seven long years are past and gane
Wha's tae ken yer dust fae mine o?

Sic transit gloria mundi: when seven years are past and gane how many of these songs will remain o?

David Campbell

Theatre Roundup

The latest blessing to be vouched us is by those selfless and indefatigable benefactors of humanity, the food technologists, is 'intelligent packaging'. This is not, however, an end to those attractive cluster-bomblets of sugar or sauce vended to the unwary in fast-food outlets; 'intelligent packaging', it seems, is wrapping material chemically treated so that warning messages will mystically become visible on it if the food inside has not been stored in correct conditions. These messages will be along the lines of: "Help! I have been tampered with!" One immediately wonders if we could have something similar for plays? For on present evidence, it would be a great help to certain theatre directors if (having decided to revive something) the manuscripts

they were rummaging around bore such legends as 'Still sparkling fresh', 'Rather past the sell-by date', or 'Now thoroughly indigestible'.

The question comes up because there has been a significant (and in some ways curious) fashion for revivals of modern Scottish plays. This is often most welcome: something as good as Chris Hannan's *Elizabeth Gordon Quinn*, glowingly revived last year by Winged Horse using much of the original cast, emphatically deserved its second airing. I feel more equivocal regarding the revival of Marcella Evaristi's *Offsky Variations* at the Tron; although admired by many, it is surely a trifle obsessive. The insoluble dilemma about putting on a revival is that the slot could have been used for new work. In this case, I would far rather have seen a new play by the same writer - particularly the really good play I am sure she is capable of writing.

Other revivals are coming. *Trade* a gripping exploration of Leith's underworld of prostitutes and rent boys was originally produced on half a frayed shoestring (for three nights only) by Oxygen House: when this searing piece of theatre is re-presented at the Traverse, it should be well worth the seeing. Another Leith play, Alan Spence's *Changed Days* is also being revived, at some expense, by the Royal Lyceum. In fairness to the Lyceum, they are probably safer reviving plays than commissioning new ones, since for at least ten years they have commissioned no new play that hasn't been dreadful. (One concedes that their dreary Scottish Molières did pull in significant numbers of those who like their panto sanitised and undemanding.) But having seen *Changed Days* at its original production in the Netherbow, I can only wish that this bland, anaemic ramble of reminiscences should have been left to moulder harmlessly. On the folder should have come up the words, "Totally stale, no trace of flavour left".

But to be fair again to the Lyceum, they have just done a very reasonable version of that greatest and most powerful of all American plays, Arthur Miller's *The Crucible*, and it was pity indeed that for want of comparatively modest funds, this large-cast production was forced to curtail its intended tour. Let me make a brief interjection. *The Crucible* is an outstanding example of a contemporary play placed in a specific historical setting, which is nevertheless vibrantly and unmistakable modern in outlook and interpretation. As such it offers a strong contrast to that Scottish genre, what might be called the "conspiracy-history" play. These are written by those lacking either the talent or inclination to find an original theme, and furthermore possessed of the desire to prove that The Establishment, whatever that is, has for centuries been engaged in a massive cover-up operation to conceal the evidence of their oppression of the Scots. Playwrights of this school are, fortunately, easy to avoid; they are instantly recognisable by the grass in their hair and mud under their collars, the consequence of ceaseless delving.

The latest offering of this kind, incidentally, was Raymond Ross's strikingly-entitled The Massacre of Tranent. (Not being one of those who are drawn to employ the services of the Lindi St Clairs of this world, I didn't go to the Brunton to see it, even though it would have been much cheaper.) For anyone who may have read my prolonged moanings on this subject in the last Chapman, however, I would point out that in the same issue, Michael Fry's review Protest · in Scotland pointed out that "on a very generous definition of dying for political beliefs", he could find only 23 examples of radical martyrs in Scotland during the 18th and early 19th centuries, with nobody at all dying for their beliefs after 1848. I suggest it is a valid point.

On now, however, to what was, beyond question, a really beguiling revival: The Cheviot, the Stag and the Black, Black Oil by Clyde Theatre. It would have been worth putting on even if only for those who, not having seen it first time round, have heard it spoken about for twenty years. Since I don't consider John McGrath to have produced anything of much value since, let me be fulsome about The Stag. It remains virtually the only successful modern Scottish play which has a significant political content, one of the few with genuine popular appeal, which people who'd never been in a theatre before could go to and really enjoy themselves, whilst also taking away some intellectual staple worth chewing over. Its targets - multi-national business, political placemen, big landowners, the clergy, etc. - were well chosen, and the satire, wittily delivered, was exquisitely satisfying. It was also brilliantly performed.

It has been said that McGrath benefited substantially from the input of various performers, who included John Bett, Alex Norton and Billy Paterson. Maybe, but I don't really think it matters. There is, for example, a theatre director - I dare not name him, mainly for fear of assassination - whom I privately suspect of having minimal directorial ability. Yet his productions are usually reasonable, often good and sometimes dazzling. How does he manage it? The answer seems to be that although he can't direct, he has a real knack for assembling talented people, 'energising' them - forgive the ghastly word - and then letting them get on with it; and this sort of knack is just as good as directorial flair. So, it would be ungenerous to deny McGrath the final

credit; for without him, after all, The Cheviot, the Stag, and the Black, Black Oil would never have seen the light of day. How has it stood up?

The wrapping, sadly, should be showing (faintly) the words, "Not really just so good as formerly"; and this is not entirely because the present production, although director by John Bett, was rather weaker than the well-remembered original. (It was played with splendid commitment and enthusiasm, but in the case of some of the younger actors, that was insufficient to make up for simple lack of experience.

No; but is not regretfully that one concludes that The Stag will not bear many revivals, and nor was that in any way a failing. Just as there is a difference between writing a newspaper article which retains its relevance for perhaps only a couple of days, and between writing a book, so there are some plays which are for their own time only. The Stag was one of these; and, believe me, we could do with a few more.

Alasdair Simpson

Pamphleteer

Douglas Dunn's Poll Tax: The Fiscal Fake (Chatto, £3.99) begins with a clear explanation of how and why the Poll Tax was dreamed up. But then his essay becomes more rambling, and much of it is, unfortunately, already dated. It's chiefly a defence of democracy, aimed at well-heeled 'waiverers', rather than those who 'can't pay, won't pay'. Dunn concludes with a poem - no bad idea in a political tract, but when it's about his observations of 'Poor People', and contains lines like 'No easy entrance/ To decent groves/ Of furtherance', its inclusion has to be questioned.

Dunn's world is remote from that described by Jim Ferguson in The Art of Catching a Bus: "ama man inthi name uv christ/ yeezll only gee mi a hoose if um pregnant". This is a world where:

thi benefit
rises ur only fur thi "deserving poor"
who ivir heard thum ask nthi form
HOW WOULD YOU DESCRIBE YOURSELF
DESERVING OR UNDESERVING?

Ferguson takes "the lanwij wiv aw got as part of livn" and shapes it into poetry - "poetry no being a purile n esoteric thing but uv ivryday life". He writes with humour and anger, and his voice demands a hearing, never more so than now, when "the military mens" heads appear from the sleeves of the politician's jacket'. The book's available at £2 from Neruda Press (51 Allison Street, Glasgow G42).

Other Tongues (ed Robert Crawford, £5.95 from Verse, Dept of English, University of St

Andrews) brings together four young Scottish poets. It opens with work by Angela McSeveney, whose territory is often that of the female body. There are poems, for example, about 'The Lump', 'Anorexia' and 'Late Period', and it's refreshing to see these common experiences made the subject of poetry. She writes movingly of her family too: "The curtains in my parents' room/ were almost always closed" are the telling final lines of 'Nightshift'.

David Kinloch's writing is epitomised by the quirky title of a prose piece, 'Paris-Forfar': he skims about, equally at home in either place, in Scots or English, celebrating "the auld alliance of words", and "planning a Scottish world" where there is "For healing: an Iona of plain space where language may draw breath".

Likewise W N Herbert is 'planning' a new Scotland, far from the kailyard of "cottars, Scots/ as marketed to Scots". His poems in English are erudite, brimming with ideas; the ones in Scots gentler, as in the 'Selkie Sang' that begins on "a lingle-back o links", or the beautifully-titled 'Morn-come-never' with its "motherie (shell-like) waurmth" and "smoorikins". The book concludes with Meg Bateman's lyrical poems in Gaelic, with English translations that convey a rare, old-fashioned quality of language. The short, simple poems are powerful in their subject matter, encompassing love and death:

is bruchdaidh a-mach mo ghaol dhut
amh-dhearg
mar na fleasgan nan laighe air an reothadh

(my love for you bursts out/ red-raw/ like the wreaths lying on the frost.)

Alchemie o the Word (Scots Glasnost, Leven £?) is a collection of Rimbaud, translated into Scots and/or English, though the Scots often has a fresher, less formal feel to it, as in Tom Hubbard's vibrant version of 'Oor burgh', which brings an 1870s poem right up to date, so you almost expect a mention of the Poll Tax in this satire on the town council. Rimbaud in Scots gives the poems a sense of internationalism, so that this "sodger loun", for example, "sleepin soun/ an gey quait-like. Twa reid holes in his briest", becomes a universal soldier. And the glimpse of a "Heid o a faun", in Tony McManus's graceful translation, could be happening in a Scottish wood, "gowd-spangelt, gem-kist", "mang the leaverie" and "crammasy flooers".

Chris Bendon's poems appear in Chapman 63, and *Ridings Writings/Scottish Gothic* (Stride, 37 Portland Street, Exeter, £4.50) offers a fuller selection of his work. The first part of the book is an autobiographical journey through his native Yorkshire, moving from his 50s childhood,

where heaven was "a beach somewhere near Bridlington", and a stamp collection "the globe stuck down in flour and water", through to an adolescence of discovering sex and poetry - both equally furtive activities. Then "My Yorkshire shrank . . ./ became like the box I kept pupae in, and forgot." But, returning as an adult, "what was in there/ buzzed at me./ Still does." Bendon's original imagery is present too in his poems about Scotland, where Glasgow high-rises are "the gossipy streets laid sideways", and in Lockerbie there is a "gap . . . in the syntax of houses".

Bendon, aware of his ambivalent status as "a sassenach", writes observantly about Scotland, in contrast to David Henderson in his novel, *The Devil's Spectacles* (Allison & Busby, £12.99). Set in the Highlands, it's about an archaeological spoof created to prop up an ailing tourist industry. The plot is thin, and the characters stereotyped, with outsiders there to 'rescue' dim-witted Highlanders. Given that the fictional hero, David, bears a great resemblance to the biographical details of the author, one can only feel sorry for the inhabitants of the Sutherland village where the real David lives.

Sights of Sinai (Sifriat Poalim Publishing House, Tel Aviv, PO Box 37068) is by an Israeli poet, Pinhas Yasur. Set in a bleak desert landscape, his poems are mainly concerned with charting the spiritual journey of a man "trampled between a heavy heaven and the earth/ trying to find the right altitude". Though the rhythms suffer somewhat in translation, the religious symbolism overlaps both Judaism and Christianity. Equally familiar is the 'Lamentation of a Mother', who wants her politicised son's soul "cleaned, ironed and nicely folded".

Michael Ivens, in *The New Divine Comedy* (Mammon Press, 12 Dartmouth Ave, Bath, £6) pursues a similar spiritual quest, though more light-heartedly. His long poem is a mix of autobiography, fantasy, and elegy for his friend Gerhardie, whose ghost he meets in Regents Park. They wander together through an underworld, meeting famous writers and mystics, visiting the 'Tavern of the Moustaches' (where Groucho Marx rubs shoulders with Shakespeare), the 'Street of Cinemas', and so on. This is done wittily enough, and there are some deeper moments, but often no more than whimsical, name-dropping self-indulgence.

As Ivens shows, "in moments of great despair/ we write and talk of the dead - so we do." This is Stephen Watts who, in *The Lava's Curl* (Grimaldi Press, North Bottomley Farm, Walsden, W Yorks, £5.95) writes poignantly of the dead, particularly in his elegy for Tsvetayeva: "This earth has bubbles they are your words". Watts' language is dense and rich and curious, describes worlds, whether imaginary, or real as London ("a lichen mapped on mild clay") or Italy ("the magnolia interiors of their convents"). Beautifully produced, this is a book to linger over, to explore with "tongue, you wild sweetmeat"; a book which reaffirms the power of language:

Should we throw out our art overboard
because our barge is plunging on a tilted
sea? All seas tilt and our alternatives
are become few and stark and desperate.

Elizabeth Burns

Catalogue

It has been said that no home is complete without a copy of The Clans by R R McIan, which provides instant chapter and verse on the history of individual Scottish clans, their stomping grounds, their tartans, their leading and most remarkable chiefs and their histories, both clan-wide and personal. The most memorable thing about this book is its portraits of individual clansmen, sporting the appropriate tartan complete with clan plant stuck on bunnet and brandishing an instrument of war. The Scolar Press have produced a similar book, The Criers and Hawkers of London, edited by and with introduction and commentary by Shawn Shesgreen. The illustrations are the famous ones by Marcellus Laroon, whose Cryes of the City of London drawne after the Life, first published in 1687, remained a best seller for a century and a half. I can see why. The drawings and engravings are remarkable for their vitality. And, unlike the McIan book, the fair sex are represented selling their baskets, strawberries, flowers or whatever. Some of the figures are unforgettable, like the drawing of Merry Andrew, a contorted jestor whose countenance suggests nothing like merriment. The Merry Fidler looked a much happier proposition. Each hawker is pictured in appropriate costume and with the tools of his trade, and in a posture which tells a story, like that of the hawker of small coals, who, to judge by the expression on his face and his general posture, finds the coals none too small. The commentary in each case is full and informed. A bit expensive at £45.00, but it is a book to keep and cherish.

Also from the Scolar Press is a must for all lovers of Scottish folk-song: the Scots Musical Museum 1787-1803 with introduction by Donald Low (2 volumes, £29.50). The Museum by James Johnson and Robert Burns, is the result of the collaboration of the poet with that altruistically motivated publisher of Scots songs. Johnson gave Burns the opportunity to devote time and energy to collecting Scottish songs by providing a

hospitable outlet for these. The publisher's humility led him to truly appreciate the qualities of his contributor, and to refrain from bowdlerisations, unlike the classy salons of Edinburgh whose appetite for the poet's work was restricted to polite verse effusions. The facsimile edition preserves Burns's notes on Scottish songs, and an appendix indicating which songs were contributed by the poet. It also preserves the sequence of songs and the integrity of the original volumes. Another important republication in the same field is Ord's Bothy Songs and Ballads with a new introduction by Alexander Fenton (John Donald £9.95). These volumes do much to ensure the continuation of the Scottish folk revival.

Norah and William Montgomerie's Traditional Scottish Nursery Rhymes (Chambers £4.99) is marvellous not merely as a bairns' book: with versions of ballads too, as a whole it is a work of art, capable of delighting a faither till the wean gets him to stop kecklan and read a thing oot.

She that gangs tae the wal
Wi an ill will,
Either the pig braks
Or the watter will spill.

That verse also has one of the best of the occasional drawings Norah contributes. The collaboration of this husband and wife team over the years has done an enormous amount to ensure that genuinely Scottish lore is handed down to the bairns.

William Donaldson says of the selection in his The Language of the People (Scots Prose from the Victorian Revival, AUP £14.50/8.95) that the language's "leading quality is a sinuous and sardonic intellectualism". Yes! Contra parochial modern nationalist academics, George Douglas Brown disavowed anti-kailyairdist intent rather intending to express "the brains" of Scots. As Dr Donaldson does: a lesson to those who visit mawkish-pawky sentimentalisms on even 1990s "Lallans". There are long slow sentences properly measured, examples of different dialects from Norn southward, characterised near all by firm control. Who knows not such is not trying to write Scots! While Betsy Whyte's Red Rowans and Wild Honey (Canongate £10.95) uses the lingua franca in narrative, that slips into a similar Scots. How Scots verse got turned into a parody of reuchness, prone to emotional clouds without civilised vocabulary, is uncertain: unless writers want the reassuring tone of a yokel sub-dialect?

The Guyanan Fred D'Aguiar's verse in Airy Hall (Chatto £5.95) is not merely taut but held together and kept in movement by an unusual pulse, as if each stanzaic element beats out a complex rhythmic pattern. He plays off dissonant sounds and dense imagery, avoids clippedness by maintaining that: his language not mellifluous but not static. His more biting sociopolitical comment achieves a compression which does not distort but makes points very straight. In *Thoughts of a Lazy Woman* (Chatto £4.99) another Guyanan, Grace Nichols, relies rather on an acute ear for cadence: a fine lyric poet. There is something wilder in the poetry of the Ghanaian Kojo Laing, *Godhorse* (Heinemann African Poets £4.95), a character of outspokenness and daring rather looser than D'Aguiar. In the same series at the same price *The Fate of Vultures* ed Zimunya, Porter and Anyidoho, is an anthology of prize-winning African poems from a BBC competition. Les A. Murray's *The Boys Who Stole the Funeral* (Carcanet £6.95) is an initially dizzying sequence of fourteen-line units (not quite the verse-novel in sonnets it's said to be). The variety of patterns and rhythms takes some getting into, but in comparison with Murray's other poetry allows greater variety of character, colour, darkness. Patrick White's *Riders in the Chariot* comes to mind: the same Australia, same sometimes unpleasant mixture, with a religious light lonelier than elsewhere in Murray. By contrast Michael Ondaatje's virtuoso *The Collected Works of Billy the Kid* (Picador £3.50) is more than mere historical evocation. It gets into the skin of this outlaw and, in the words of Harper Lee in *To Kill a Mockingbird*, takes a walk around in it. *The Cinnamon Peeler*, his Selected Poems, is £4.99 from the same publisher and represents a wide variety of moods and observations, including of Ondaatje's unusual Indian background.

Still impressive, ever to be lamented, Frances Horovitz (1938-83) was a real lyric poet remarkable above her contemporaries and associates. Bloodaxe (with Enitharmon) happily republish her *Collected Poems* at £7.95. They also do *Poems Before and After* (£7.95), collected English translations of the not unknown Miroslav Holub. Cf. too *Selected Poems* of John Heath-Stubbs (Carcanet £5.95), and those of the Sanskrit poet/playwriter Kalidasa (who lived a normal span somewhere between the dates 900 and 1450 AD): *The Loom of Time* (Penguin £4.99). *Victorian Fairy Tales* ed Michael Patrick Hearn (Canongate £12.95 hardback!) is an anthology of 19th C. texts. *The Virago Book of Love Poetry* ed Wendy Mulford (Virago, £6.99), all by women is by no means the reheat many such books are. Nor is *Kissing the Rod*, 17th century women's verse (Virago £14.95), figureheaded by Germaine Greer (&c.). This reveals that what one poet calls "the insulting sex" (she means the male!) has few monopolies: by no means routine, well worth doing. M S Lumsden's *Affirmations* (AUP £9.50)

is amateur semiscots verse by a nice lady.

From John Donald, the photographer Ian Torrance's *Edinburgh Through the Lens* (£14.95) finds acute angles but remains a shade conservative: worth checking. Donald's chronicling of that city continues with Joyce Wallace's *Further Traditions of Trinity and Leith* and Malcolm Cant's *Sciennes and the Grange*, both £7.50 and stunningly handsome, full of persons, antiquities, histories. Derek Cooper's *Hebridean Connection* (Fontana £4.99) is efficient journalism from a well-known broadcaster: on a topic more open to discussion than most. Why? Francis Salvesen's *Journal of a Student at Arms* (Warrior Enterprises, Spruce (sic!) House, 38 Kingswood Road SW2 4JH, £4.95) is a memoir of Sandhurst days resembling the yearbook with which the ole skool tai is issued.

Unlike Michael Coveney's *The Citz* (Nick Hern Books, £14.95/£8.95). With a roguish drowning wave Giles Havergal mounted his Hamlet-in-G-Strings at Glasgow Citizens Theatre in 1969. The place was due to be closed, anyway: the paint-merchant chairman of the committee declaring it needed an in-house writer (he named Ben Travers: Oh, Calamity!). But by a combination of crassness and flagrant theatricality Giles has kept the place going for 21 years, and some of his early 1970s casts even learned to act (which once seemed impossible). Where else in Scotland would you think of as congruent with the images in Penguin's *The Soviet Arts Poster* (£14.99) full of the most startling and brilliant images, A3 format. Curiously enough the late 17th century can nowhere be conjured better than by the Citizens. Which nonetheless lacked the imagination to put on new Scottish plays, like the complainants who said the Citizens should do them wholesale. Theatres is gey strynge airts!

Lewis Grassic Gibbon's *A Scots Quair* is in one Penguin volume, £5.99, J.M. Barrie's *Farewell Miss Julie Logan* are the latest additions to join the ASLS/Scottish Academic Press's Scottish Classics series, £4.95. Penguin's *The Portable Malcolm Cowley* (£7.99) is worth noting for Cowley is a great critic. From the Canadian Robertson Davies, happily remembered no less for outstanding novels than for his year as Fellow in Scotland, comes a near comparable *A Voice from the Attic* (Penguin £5.99), acute critical thinking. Another pair like in kind are *Poems and Shorter Writings* by J. Joyce, £14.99, and *Ground Work* by the American Paul Auster, £5.99, both Faber but not necessarily comparable. Ivan Tolstoy's *The Knowledge and the Power* (Canongate £15.95) is another impressive study in the History of Science by the extremely distinguished biographer of James Clerk Maxwell.

NOTES ON CONTRIBUTORS

Donald Adamson: has taught English abroad, now lives in Dalbeattie, writing and editing EFL textbooks. Winner, 1985 Radio Clyde Poetry Prize.

Elizabeth Burns: poet, founder member of Stramullion women's publishing house in Edinburgh.

Angus Calder: Principal organiser of *Writing Together*, Glasgow 1990's literary carnival; Open University lecturer.

David Campbell: formerly of BBC Schools department in Edinburgh.

Ken Cockburn: Edinburgh-based writer & arts administrator. The present story was written for the Paupers Carnival Theatre's *Desirable Residents*.

Robert Crawford: Lecturer in Modern Scottish Literarure at the University of St Andrews. His collections of poetry include *A Scottish Assembly* (1990)

George Garson: shipwright, journalist & writer since retiring from Senior Lectureship at Glasgow School of Art in 1984.

David Gill: b Chislehurst 1934. Has spent much time abroad; published several books of poetry, recently *The White Raven*, trans. from Ondra Lyschorsky.

Mary Gladstone: Galloway born poet, writer of fiction, plays and journalism. Now lives in Sutherland.

W N Herbert: recent PhD thesis on MacDiarmid to be published by OUP. Edits *Gairfish* along with Richard Price.

Mary McCabe: Writer & Careers Counsellor. Published in Germany and Scotland, plays broadcast in Germany & Switzerland. Currently writing the official Strathclyde R. C. history of the Capital of Culture events.

Ranald Macdonald: b 1955, studied Literature, Speech & Drama; has worked as a Waldorf School teacher. Also writes stories & plays.

Stuart McHardy: b Dundee 1947. Formerly a professional musician, now a writer & broadcaster currently working on a collection of whisky smuggling stories *Tales o the Peatreek* due this autumn.

Christine McNeill: b Vienna, lived in England since 1970. Formerly ESL tutor, but now lives and writes in Norfolk. In Bloodaxe collecton *New Women Poets*.

Edwin Morgan: Er . . . weren't you paying attention?

Ken Morrice: Psychiatrist practising in Aberdeen. His sixth collection of poetry, *The Scampering Marmoset*, is reviewed in this issue.

Uilleam Neill: once teacher and now full-time poet. Writes in English, Scots and Gaelic. Cassette *Poems in Three Leids* recently issued by *Scotsoun*.

Jenny Robertson: poet, playwright and children's author living in Edinburgh. Her book *Beyond the Border* is in the *Chapman* New Writing Series.

Alasdair Simpson: Edinburgh journalist & scriptwriter, until recently theatre critic of the TESS.

Judy Steel: Prominent member of the Borders arts community and active Liberal Democrat.

Fred Urquhart: prominent Scottish short story writer and novelist, critic and ex-literary editor. Lives in Sussex.

Roderick Watson: Graduate of Aberdeen & Cambridge, now Senior Lecturer at the University of Stirling. Author, *The Literature of Scotland*, *MacDiarmid*, and *The Poetry of Norman MacCaig*; co-author *The Penguin Book of the Bicycle* and writer of poetry.